The Brigadier

By the same author

Far from a Gentleman
Anything but a Soldier
Steeplechasing (with John Skeaping)
The Theory and Practice of Flat Race Riding
From Start to Finish

The Brigadier

John Hislop

SECKER & WARBURG

LONDON

First published in England 1973 by
Martin Secker & Warburg Limited
14 Carlisle Street, London W1V 6NN

Copyright © John Hislop 1973
Reprinted before publication
2nd Reprint 1974

SBN: 436 19700 6

Filmset and printed in Great Britain by
Cox & Wyman Ltd
London, Fakenham & Reading

To Jean
My wife, and partner in Brigadier Gerard

'I have a spirit like a slip of steel, for
the more you bend it the higher it springs'
The Adventures of Gerard, A. Conan Doyle

CONTENTS

Part One

Part Two

Part Three

LIST OF ILLUSTRATIONS

PART ONE

1 *Prelude to the Story*

The story of Brigadier Gerard begins a long time ago.

From childhood I had been drawn to racing and at my preparatory school the riding mistress, Miss Clay, appreciating my dedication, used to tell me about that brilliant mare Pretty Polly; how she carried all before her and after her only two defeats – in the Prix du Conseil Municipal and the Ascot Gold Cup – she hung her head in sadness. So Pretty Polly became, and has remained, my equine heroine and inspiration throughout my racing life.

She even found her way into the pages of my mother's Bible, in the form of a book-marker I made out of a cigarette card upon which Pretty Polly was featured.

Many years later the theme was translated into reality when I went to work as a pupil of Victor Gilpin at Clarehaven, where his father, Peter Purcell Gilpin – who coincidentally shared my birthdate of 12 December – had trained Pretty Polly. Forty years ago, when I first joined the stable, the aura of Pretty Polly still shone strongly, if invisibly, over Clarehaven.

Pretty Polly's dam, Admiration, was bought by Major Eustace Loder as a yearling for 510 guineas. On pedigree she had little to recommend her, for not a single winner of any distinction is to be found in her tail female line for many generations.

Her ancestress Boadicea (by Alexander–Brunette, by Amaranthus) won several small races under the name of Tarporley Lass; then, reverting to her former name Boadicea, she carried the celebrated huntsman of the Pytchley Hounds, Charles King, with courage and distinction, just as her full brother, Benvolio, had carried the Master, Sir Charles Knightly.

At the close of the hunting season of 1819, Boadicea was sold to Lady Grosvenor, after having been covered by the St Leger winner Orville.

In 1820, Boadicea foaled a filly, named Etiquette, who in due course bred Maid of Honor, by Champion. The significance of Maid of Honor in Admiration's pedigree is that she is the ancestress of both the sire and dam of Admiration. Saraband, sire of Admiration, is out of Highland Fling, out of Masquerade, out of Burlesque, out of Maid of Honor, who is also the sixth dam of Admiration's dam Gaze.

Saraband (by Muncaster), sire of Admiration, was a useful racehorse, winning two Ascot Biennials, the Chesterfield Cup, the Rous Memorial Stakes and other races, but Gaze (by Thuringian Prince) ran once – unplaced in a selling race.

It would seem that something was thought of Admiration as a two-year-old, since the second of the only two races she contested that season was the important Richmond Stakes at Goodwood. However, this idea, if it ever existed, did not bear fruit, as she ran till she was five, winning two minor handicaps in Ireland and being placed second in England and several times in Ireland, in races of little or no account.

Following this modest career on the racecourse, Admiration developed into a broodmare of immortal fame, founding a line which was destined to gather and maintain distinction throughout the world. She bred thirteen foals in thirteen years, nine of them winners and her daughters brought further notable success to the family.

The winning colts out of Admiration were Aderno (by Laveno), Admirable Crichton (by Isinglass), Admiral Hawke (by Gallinule) and Coriander (by Spearmint). Aderno was moderate, but the others were able to win good-class races at courses such as Newmarket, Goodwood and Sandown, if appreciably below classic standard.

The first filly from Admiration was Veneration II (by Laveno), who won a race worth £440, a decent sum for 1902, at Sandown, and produced Craganour (by Desmond) who finished first in the sensational Derby of 1913, but was disqualified in favour of Aboyeur, also a son of Desmond. At that time Desmond's stock were being criticised on the grounds that they did not stay. After the race one observer was heard to remark: 'They say the Desmonds don't stay and now he's got two Derby winners in one year!'

Then came Pretty Polly (by Gallinule), followed by her less distinguished full sisters Adula, Adora and Miranda, and her half sisters Miramonde (by Desmond) and Addenda (by Spearmint). The best race-mare of Pretty Polly's sisters and half sisters was Adula, who won the Park Hill Stakes; and she, together with Miranda and Veneration II, became good broodmares, founding distinctive, successful lines of their own. But it is with Pretty Polly that this story is concerned.

Pretty Polly's sire Gallinule, a half brother to the St James's Palace Stakes winner Pioneer (by Galopin), was a dark chesnut, 16 hands, by

Pretty Polly (W. Lane up)

Isonomy out of Moorhen, by Hermit. He had a prominent white blaze, an odd-looking white patch on the near side of his face, from the nostril to just above the start of the cheek-bone, and four white socks, those behind coming almost up to his hocks. In general appearance there was a good deal of Gallinule about Pretty Polly, and there seems to be a tendency in the Admiration family for the mares to throw to the stallions with which they are mated. This certainly has been so with Brigadier Gerard's dam, La Paiva.

Gallinule was inbred 3 × 4 to Stockwell (The Baron–Pocahontas), that is to say, Stockwell occurred once in the third remove of his pedigree and once in the fourth remove. The mating of Gallinule with Pretty Polly's dam Admiration produced, through the latter, an additional line of Stockwell and one of his full brother, Rataplan. It is possible that this concentration of the important influence of The Baron and Pocahontas, respectively sire and dam of Stockwell and Rataplan, may have had something to do with the brilliance of Pretty Polly, since the poor record of the tail female line for so many generations does not suggest it as a source of racing ability.

The Stallion Register for 1904 describes Gallinule as having won the National Breeders Produce Stakes, at Sandown, 'and many other races', a somewhat flattering statement, since from a total of twenty-one starts over four seasons, he won only two other races, both at two years. This disappointing record after a promising beginning was due to Gallinule starting to break blood vessels, for, as his performance in the National Breeders Stakes shows, he had considerable ability. Fortunately, the breaking of blood vessels is a weakness which does not appear to have been inherited by Pretty Polly, as I cannot recall any member of the line suffering from it.

Gallinule, who was owned by Captain Greer, began his stud career at Brownstown, the Curragh, at the modest fee of 9 guineas, which later rose to 200. He became a successful sire, mostly of sprinters and milers, though his winners include Wildfowler, who won the St Leger.

Pretty Polly was foaled in 1901 and was brought up at the Eyrefield Lodge Stud, Newbridge, Co. Kildare, which Major Eustace Loder had bought from the Linde family. The stud was managed by Mr Noble Johnson, who held the position till his death, first with Major Eustace Loder and then, after the latter died, with Lieut-Col. Giles Loder. Noble Johnson was succeeded by Peter Burrell, who later became Director of the National Stud. The Eyrefield Lodge was destined to enjoy a long spell of success, which held up remarkably well.

Pretty Polly was broken at Eyrefield as a yearling and, as related by the late Edward Moorehouse in his obituary of Pretty Polly in the *Bloodstock Breeders' Review* of 1931, from an account of the incident given him by Noble Johnson, she might have met her end during the process:

When out on the Curragh one day, being driven in long reins, Pretty Polly got loose, and ran round the top of a sand quarry forty feet deep. She raced along a narrow path, on one side of which was the quarry and on the other a high stone wall, and had been round twice before she allowed herself to be caught.

The first time that Pretty Polly showed any sign of the brilliance which she produced later on the racecourse was of an equally unprecedented nature. To quote from Moorehouse:

In December, not long after this escapade (when she got loose) Pretty Polly took part of her own free will in a 'rough gallop' over three furlongs with some yearlings that were being got ready for racing early the following season. 'Polly' was merely out for an airing, but Mr Johnson told Anthony*, who was riding her, to go down to where the other yearlings were to start their spin and look on. When 'Polly' saw her stable companions set off, she overpowered Anthony, and went after them. At the end of three furlongs, where Mr Johnson was standing, she was leading, and went on for a considerable distance before Anthony could pull her up. In that, her first 'race' she carried about 10 st, the others were carrying only 8 st. One of them was Vervel who won a race the following April, and ran second in the 'Patriotic' at Baldoyle and in the Grand Prize at the Curragh. Her performance in the unauthorised gallop caused everyone at Eyrefield to wonder what manner of a filly she was. Shortly after it she was sent to Newmarket to be trained by Mr Peter Gilpin, who had recently moved thither from Dorsetshire, and built 'Clarehaven' near the old toll bar on the Bury Road.

Clarehaven was called after the horse of that name whom Peter Gilpin had trained to win the Cesarewitch of 1900. The establishment is now owned by Mr David Robinson, who pulled down the old house and built a modern one in its place; but the yard and paddock is much the same as it was and is one of the best training stables in the country.

Victor Gilpin recently described Pretty Polly to me as 'a strong, beautifully made polo pony, about 15.2'. She was a dark chesnut with a handsome, intelligent head and a nice temperament.

When she arrived at Clarehaven she worked sluggishly and did not impress Peter Gilpin greatly. 'The first time I saw her in a paddock at Eyrefield Lodge she struck me as being almost too powerful. If anybody had told me the filly I was looking at was going to develop into a great racemare I should have laughed,' he once remarked to Moorehouse.

Before Pretty Polly appeared in public she showed that she possessed at least a measure of ability, as a result of a gallop with a two-year-old colt, Delaunay (Fortunio–Pet, by Peter), who had just won, first time out, by five lengths at Manchester. Two others made up the starters in the gallop, one being a two-year-old gelding named Addlestone (Alloway–Agnes Sarum, by Adieu). Delaunay was set to give 23 lb to Pretty Polly and 14 lb

* Probably Algy Anthony.

to Addlestone. Pretty Polly still carried a lot of flesh, attempts to make her sweat and remove some of it having failed. Despite her lack of racing condition she hung on well in the gallop and finished less than a length behind Delaunay, well ahead of the others.

Since Pretty Polly was receiving 23 lb her performance did not amount to much, but at least it showed that she was waking up and gave promise of improvement.

Delaunay, after whom I named La Paiva's colt by Donore, turned out a pretty good horse, winning seventeen races, including the July Cup, while Addlestone won thrice as a two-year-old and once the following year.

Pretty Polly's first race was the British Dominion Plate at Sandown on 27 June 1903. The previous day, also at Sandown, Delaunay ran and won easily, which was a good omen, but despite racecourse rumours of her having done a good gallop with Delaunay, Pretty Polly found no great favour with punters and started at 6 to 1. Favourite for the race was Sir John Thursby's colt John o'Gaunt (Isinglass–La Flèche, by St Simon), who was destined to finish second in the Derby and gain immortality as the sire of Swynford.

In the days before the introduction of starting stalls, and now on the occasions when the gate is used, there is usually a fairly considerable pause between the horses beginning to line up and the 'off'. Thus, after the field for the British Dominion Plate had been at the gate barely a minute before the barrier was raised, hardly anyone among the spectators was aware that the race was on. When they realised it was in progress, they saw one of the runners so far ahead of the others that they presumed there had been a false start and that at any instant the red flag would signal it. But the start was a fair one and the horse far ahead of the others was Pretty Polly, who had shot out of the gate and was in the process of increasing her lead with every stride. At the post she was about a hundred yards in front, which the photograph of the finish confirms, though Judge Robinson, whom an unkind racegoer pronounced in need of a braille racecard, gave the distance as ten lengths.

In second place came the filly Vergia, a neck in front of John o'Gaunt, ridden by his owner's brother, Mr George Thursby – later Sir George Thursby – who as an amateur had the rare distinction of being placed second in the Derby twice, on John o'Gaunt and Picton.

Pretty Polly was ridden by Trigg, known on the Turf as Hell Fire Jack. Looking neither to right nor to left, Trigg made the best of his way home and, on returning to the weighing room, remarked that Pretty Polly was slowing down as the winning post was approached. 'Slowing down!' George Thursby exclaimed, 'As she was leading by a hundred yards it is hardly surprising.' Moorehouse writes, and Victor Gilpin has told me the same, that the extraordinary improvement made by Pretty Polly between her trial and first race was attributed by Peter Gilpin to the fact that, on her journey from Newmarket to Sandown in the great heat prevailing at the time, the sweat poured off her, which had never happened before.

The effect of this lesson was not lost on the Gilpins: during my time with Victor we always sweated lazy horses and it proved an effective way of getting them fit. A typical case was the Ascot Stakes winner Bonny Boy II (Comrade–Basse Pointe, by Simonian), who always worked so sluggishly that he was tailed off in every gallop in which he took part.

Pretty Polly then proceeded to win her remaining eight races as a two-year-old: the National Breeders Produce Stakes at Sandown, the Mersey Stakes at Liverpool, the Champagne Stakes at Doncaster, the Manchester Autumn Breeders Foal Plate, and the Cheveley Park Stakes, the Middle Park Plate, the Criterion Stakes and the Moulton Stakes, all at Newmarket.

In each case she won in a canter and in the National Breeders Stakes and Champagne Stakes started at the remarkably generous prices, respectively, of 2 to 1 and 11 to 10. Halsey rode her at Sandown and Liverpool and W. Lane in the remainder of her races that season.

Raced for three further seasons, Pretty Polly won twenty-two races during her career, these including the One Thousand Guineas, Oaks, St Leger, Park Hill Stakes, Coronation Cup (twice), Champion Stakes and the Jockey Club Cup.

Considering the exigencies of travel between England and France in those days, and the consequent detrimental effect on the running of racehorses subjected to it, it seems surprising that Pretty Polly was sent to run in the Prix du Conseil Municipal, one and half miles, at Longchamp in October, as a three-year-old, having already had six races that season.

Questioned as to this decision before the race, Eustace Loder replied that the chief reason was that he wanted to see Pretty Polly beat the best horses in France, as she had accounted for the best in England, adding, 'but I would rather forfeit £40,000 than see her beaten'. At that time there were some good horses in France, notably Ajax (by Flying Fox), who was to prove such a great influence on thoroughbred breeding in France, Gouvernant, Caius and Macdonald II.

As it happened, Ajax was taken out of the race owing to leg trouble, Gouvernant and Caius because their owner, M. Edmond Blanc, did not think that they had the slightest chance of beating Pretty Polly, leaving only Macdonald II as an apparently worthy French representative.

Accompanying Pretty Polly to the post was the English colt Zinfandel, who as a result of the death of his breeder, Colonel Harry McCalmont, was automatically struck out of all his classic engagements, a rule which was later and rightly done away with. Zinfandel, then a four-year-old, was the best colt in England; a handsome chesnut, he was by Persimmon out of Medora, by Bend Or, and his many victories include the Coronation Cup and the Ascot Gold Cup. He was undoubtedly superior to his contemporary Rock Sand, who won the Triple Crown.

Pretty Polly had a bad journey from Boulogne to Paris, her train being frequently held up and shunted, which must have taken a good deal out of her. Added to this the going was very heavy. These factors contributed to bring about Pretty Polly's first defeat and she went under by two and a half lengths to the outsider Presto II, to whom she was giving 10 lb, Zinfandel taking third place, half a length behind Pretty Polly. Danny Maher, who rode Pretty Polly, attributed her defeat to the fact that she was not a true stayer and that, as a result, the heavy going found her out.

Stamina in top-class horses is difficult to define, because horses of outstanding ability can win at any distance. As Alec Head, trainer of Riverman, who ran third to Brigadier Gerard and Parnell in the King George VI and Queen Elizabeth Stakes, observed after the race, 'distance makes no difference to a horse like Brigadier Gerard'. It is a matter of deciding the distance at which a horse can show his absolute best. When raced outside his absolute best distance, in disadvantageous circumstances, against horses of the highest calibre racing over their absolute best distance, defeat can come about.

The fact that in the Coronation Cup the following year Pretty Polly was able to beat Zinfandel in a canter by three lengths, suggests that the journey was probably the true cause of her downfall in Paris.

But Danny Maher always stuck to his opinion that a supreme test of stamina would find a chink in Pretty Polly's armour and, after she had beaten Bachelor's Button, ridden by Maher, for the Jockey Club Cup (two and a quarter miles) as a four-year-old, he declared that Bachelor's Button would reverse the form over the extra two furlongs of the Ascot Gold Cup the following year, if the pair met in it.

Maher's forecast proved correct, for Bachelor's Button did beat Pretty Polly in the Ascot Gold Cup, but may have been lucky to do so. A few days before the race a wart on Pretty Polly's belly had to be lanced. This may have upset her, since she was nervous and fretful in the paddock and did not want to go out on the course, which was quite out of character and suggests that she felt that she was not in a state to do herself full justice.

In the race, Pretty Polly did not have the best of runs, being carried out of her ground by the tiring Achilles, and in the last hundred yards she was caught and passed by Bachelor's Button, who won by a length.

Peter Gilpin attributed her defeat to her jockey, Dillon, not carrying out his instructions. He could well be right since, in theory, Dillon would have done better to make the fullest use of Pretty Polly's speed by holding her up to the last possible moment, instead of hitting the front so far from home. Dillon was a good jockey, but did not possess the superb artistry and judgment of Maher. One cannot help but feel that, had Maher been in the saddle, he might have proved himself wrong.

2 The Start of a Career

The chief owner at Clarehaven in my day was Lieut-Col Giles Loder, a nephew of Pretty Polly's owner Major Eustace Loder, from whom he had inherited the Eyrefield Stud. Though from time to time mares of different female lines had been introduced to Eyrefield, only the line founded by Pretty Polly's dam, Admiration, survived; the other lines faded out as a result of failing to produce stock of sufficiently high standard to merit keeping in the stud.

From the family of Admiration and, particularly through the Pretty Polly branch, came a stream of winners and high-class horses. Of those who preceded me, such as the brilliant fillies Arabella, Golden Silence and Sister Anne, I heard from Victor Gilpin, his head lad Binnie, and George Cracknell, the travelling lad. Also from some of the senior stablemen, notably Mahoney, by then old, bent and toothless, who used to 'do' Pretty Polly. So that my imagination became fired by the fame and romance of this brilliant family.

During my time at Clarehaven no horse of classic standard came from the Pretty Polly family to the stable, though they included some good ones. The best was Colorado Kid (Colorado–Baby Polly, by Spearmint–Pretty Polly), winner of the Kempton Jubilee, Royal Hunt Cup, Chesterfield Cup and Doncaster Cup, in succession. He was no beauty, being back at the knee and having bent hocks, but a tough, game horse, lazy at home though a real battler on the racecourse. He was a smallish, bright bay horse, with a delightful temperament and had a habit of racing with his tongue out, as Brigadier Gerard sometimes did.

Colorado Kid was an unimpressive, shuffling goer in his slow paces, but when set alight could really stretch out, as I found when I rode him one day and he was roused by a loose horse coming up behind him with the bridle, which had come off but remained attached by the martingale, clanking on the ground.

Another good horse, a four-year-old when I arrived, was Christopher

Robin (Phalaris–Dutch Mary, by William the Third–Pretty Polly). A handsome, virtually black horse, with forelegs typical of many sons and daughters of Phalaris, being rather back at the knee, Christopher Robin was a good but moody horse. As a two-year-old he had run second in the Imperial Produce Stakes to Roral (Abbots Trace–Dew of June, by Polymelus).

The story of Roral is interesting. Harry Cottrill, his trainer, a superb judge not only of horses but of dogs and cattle, was asked to judge at Islington, in those days the most important horse show of the year. He gave the championship to a thoroughbred as against a hunter-bred horse and for this decision was criticised by the hunting faction of the Committee, who voiced the opinion that he was biased in favour of a thoroughbred, because he was a flat race trainer. Cottrill was so incensed by this that he announced that not only would he never judge at the show again, but he would produce a thoroughbred who would win at the show and go on to win on the flat. This he did with Roral.

In his second season, Christopher Robin won the St James's Palace Stakes at Ascot, beating the hot favourite Rustom Pasha (Son-in-Law–Cos, by Orby), who later won the Eclipse Stakes and Champion Stakes. Christopher Robin did not win at four, but went under by a short head to Racedale (Buchan–Perfection, by Orby) in the Kempton Jubilee.

During my time with Victor Gilpin at Clarehaven and later at Michel Grove, near Findon in Sussex, four other descendants of Pretty Polly stand out in my mind.

The full brother and sister Annabel and Berwick, by Blandford out of Arabella, by Buchan out of Polly Flinders, by Polymelus out of Pretty Polly. Both were good looking, Annabel a hard bay of the hue typical of their sire Blandford (Swynford–Blanche, by White Eagle) and many of his stock, Berwick a brown; each had a blaze. They were good two-year-olds, but neither trained on. I sometimes used to ride Berwick, a light-actioned, kind, sensitive and highly strung colt, a beautiful ride in a gallop, though restless when in the string or hacked away from it.

The others were the half brother and sister Golden Eagle (by Fairway) and Tip the Wink (by Tetratema) out of Golden Silence, by Swynford out of Molly Desmond, by Desmond out of Pretty Polly. This is the branch to which Brigadier Gerard belongs, as his fourth dam is Molly Desmond.

Golden Eagle was a beautiful chestnut colt of great ability, but impetuous. As a two-year-old, he ran second to Glen Loan (Loaningdale–Abbot's Glen, by Abbots Trace) in the Imperial Produce Stakes and was runner-up in the Criterion Stakes at Newmarket and a race at York.

The following season, as a result of Joe Marshall, the stable jockey, taking a great deal of trouble over him, Golden Eagle settled down and was very well tried for the Two Thousand Guineas. Tragically, he got cast in his box, cracked his pelvis and never raced again. He recovered sufficiently to be able to go to stud, where he had limited opportunity and died comparatively young, but has the distinction of having sired Gilded, the third dam of Huntercombe (Derring-Do–Ergina, by Fair Trial), winner of the Middle Park Stakes, Nunthorpe Stakes, July Cup and other important sprint races.

An interesting aspect of Gilded is that she is inbred to Pretty Polly, who is the fourth dam of her dam, Overture, and the third dam of her sire, Golden Eagle.

Another inbreeding to Pretty Polly exists in Dossa Dossi, winner of the Italian One Thousand Guineas and Oaks. She was by Spike Island (ex Molly Desmond, ex Pretty Polly) out of Delleana (ex Duccia di Buoninsegna, ex Dutch Mary, ex Pretty Polly), dam of Donatello II.

Tip the Wink, a beautiful, brown filly, was a good two-year-old, winning the Newmarket Spring Two-Year-Old Stakes, the Caterham Stakes at Epsom and the Bretby Stakes at Newmarket. She did not train on and ran only once, unplaced, as a three-year-old. Tip the Wink is the third dam of the Musidora Stakes and Nassau Stakes winner Catherine Wheel (by Roan Rocket), who visits Brigadier Gerard in 1973. This mating gives a line breeding to Molly Desmond.

After spending nine years with Victor Gilpin I became fond of the Pretty Polly family and deeply interested in their characteristics. Their chief quality, if they had any racing merit, was speed. No matter how much stamina the stallion with which one of the Pretty Polly line mares was mated, the offspring invariably possessed speed, if it was any good at all.

At that time, certainly of those who came to our stable, few of them stayed a mile and a half, exceptions being Golden Silence and Sister Anne, both of whom were placed in the Oaks. Though Colorado Kid won the Doncaster Cup (two and a quarter miles), this was a two-horse race, run at a crawl.

They tended to have the tail set on low and, sometimes, to have bent or curby hocks, as had Sister Anne; this factor appears to be carried as a recessive in the line.

They were often highly strung and most of them required only a light preparation to bring them to their best. Probably for reasons of temperament, a number failed to train on. A few of the fillies were jady and had delicate constitutions. As a whole, they had sound, clean forelegs.

On the other hand, in Italy under the exacting regimen of the great Federico Tesio, the family went from strength to strength, winning at twelve furlongs and over and proving tough, courageous racehorses. The same was to be the case in France, some years later, when the unreliable fillies Mauretania (by Tetratema) and her dam Lady Maureen (Spearmint –Molly Desmond) founded the branch in the Rothschild Stud at Meautry, from which has emerged a stream of brilliant racehorses, among them Guersant, Ocarina, Flute Enchantée and Violoncelle.

As time went on, the trend of the best representatives of the Pretty Polly family to appear in studs other than Eyrefield became more marked. After the war, the Dunchurch Lodge Stud produced the St Leger winner Premonition (Precipitation–Trial Ground, by Fair Trial); while Supreme Court (Persian Gulf or Precipitation–Forecourt, by Fair Trial), who won the first running of the King George VI and Queen Elizabeth Stakes, introduced to mark the Festival of Britain, came from the Woolton House Stud; St Paddy (Aureole–Edie Kelly, by Bois Roussel) won the Derby, St Leger and Eclipse Stakes for the Sassoon Studs, and Psidium (Pardal– Dinarella, by Niccolo dell'Arca) gave the family another victory in the Derby, having been bred by the Dollanstown Stud. All of these trace to Pretty Polly in the female line.

This phenomenon is common. After a number of generations on the same land families often deteriorate, reviving under a different environment and as a result of being mated with sires bred in other countries.

My objective at that period of my life was, eventually, to become a flat race trainer. I was in no particular hurry, since such a move would have curtailed, if not put an end to, my riding as an amateur on the flat and over obstacles. At the same time I began to take a close interest in breeding, and there grew in my mind the ambition that one day I would own a mare from the Pretty Polly family.

The war finished my career in a racing stable, but military service never succeeded in divorcing me from the Turf. At every opportunity I went racing and kept in close touch with racing affairs and, in the early years of the war, when jumping was still going, I had a few rides, and a couple of winners.

My last ride of this era proved an important step in my career as a breeder, since it resulted in a fall which kept me out of action for a year and a half. With much time on my hands, I read as many books on breeding as I could lay hands on, studied Bruce Lowe's theories and Vuillier's

Dosage system, writing out innumerable pedigrees of important winners and working out the trends which these revealed.

Many of the theories I studied had scientific loopholes, and more than a few ideas I formed about breeding proved unsound, but the time spent on the subject was not wasted, giving me a basic knowledge of pedigrees and bloodlines, which has proved of help and interest ever since.

Breeding racehorses is largely a matter of practical experience, intelligent appreciation of changing trends and influences, trial and error, a basic knowledge of genetics and of pastures, together with luck. While luck can never be ignored, it is a fact that the harder anyone works at any subject the luckier he becomes.

The trouble is that without the right guidance this accumulated information takes a long time to acquire, and the cost of the essential lessons of trial and error sometimes results in the financial sinking of the breeder before he can reach the shore or success and solvency. Had I, twenty-five years ago, possessed the knowledge and experience acquired over the years, I would have saved thousands of pounds lost through working on unsound principles and making avoidable mistakes.

My first broodmare, Orama (Diophon–Cantelupe, by Amadis) was bought privately by me during the war, but she did not come from the Pretty Polly family; she traced to Whinbloom (Galeazzo–Furze Bush, by Fitz James), a branch of the No. 1 Bruce Lowe family, which has produced some good winners, among them Nearula (Two Thousand Guineas), Mesa (French One Thousand Guineas) and the King George VI and Queen Elizabeth Stakes winner Vimy.

Orama did well, breeding a great many winners, the best being Beausite (by Bold Archer), whom she produced before I bought her. Beausite won the Falmouth Stakes, ran second in the One Thousand Guineas and fourth in the Oaks, and is the third dam of Waterloo (One Thousand Guineas). Later Orama threw Respite (by Flag of Truce), dam of Nearula (by Nasrullah) and Drum Beat (by Fair Trial), a good sprinter who became a successful sire in South Africa, and Oceana (by Colombo), sold by me to Stanley Wootton, who from her bred the outstanding Australian racehorses and sires, Todman and Noholme, both by Star Kingdom (known in England as Star King).

The first of my early errors was, instead of keeping only Orama and developing her family, I bought more mares, first on my own account and later in partnership with the late Pat Dyke Dennis. As a result, to pay expenses, the daughters of Orama were sold and a good line was lost to me.

My partnership with Pat Dennis came about because I had no stud of my own and by going in with him I was able to keep mares at his stud. To start with, they were at Stansty Park, Wrexham. After the war Pat moved to Ireland and founded the Greenmount Stud, in County Limerick. A first-class horsemaster, he looked after the mares and young stock really well, the land was good and we bred our fair share of winners. The yearlings were sold at public auction.

The second mistake I made was not appreciating the different policy necessary for breeding yearlings for sale, as compared with breeding horses to race oneself. The two operations bear practically no relation to each other, since the average yearling buyer wants only well-grown, handsome yearlings, likely to win as two-year-olds. A promising middle-distance classic prospect will naturally sell well, but this type of yearling often does not compare favourably in looks with the more forward, sprinting type of yearling and, in consequence, the latter usually shows a better profit on the cost of production, the classic-bred yearling being expensive to breed.

Our mistake was that, with limited capital, we were attempting to breed middle-distance stock, but not of classic calibre, resulting in yearlings which few buyers wanted; and if they did, the price had to be modest.

The most successful commercial breeders, of whom the late George Harris was a supreme example, never set their sights too high. They usually had a couple of stallions of their own, wisely bought at a reasonable price and of a type whose stock was likely to appeal to buyers, chose their mares on the same principles and were content with consistent, comparatively modest profits, as opposed to trying to breed a Derby winner. Occasionally they came up with a top-class winner, as when George Harris's Ballykisteen Stud produced the One Thousand Guineas winner Happy Laughter (Royal Charger–Bray Melody, by Coup de Lyon), but so long as they showed a steady profit they worried little about prestige.

Commercial breeders with an over-ambitious target are liable to lose a great deal of money and, as regards the prestige of breeding classic winners, are up against the huge, unseen portion of the iceberg, in the shape of private breeders with a large capital behind them.

The immense advantage in taxation recently enjoyed by breeders in Eire over their counterparts in England has put them in a position with which English commercial breeders cannot hope to compete, because the latter are unable to afford the top-class nominations and breeding stock which the Irish are now in a position to acquire.

3   *Brazen Molly's Purchase and History*

Just after the war, the chance to buy a mare tracing to Pretty Polly came my way. This was Brazen Molly, a young, barren bay mare by Horus out of Molly Adare, by Phalaris out of Molly Desmond, by Desmond out of Pretty Polly. She was a little plain, but well made, lengthy, with good, clean limbs, plenty of room to carry a foal, wide quarters, a bold intelligent head and was a strong, easy mover. Unbroken, because of the war, she had had a foal, which died, but there seemed no reason why she should not breed again.

On paper she read well, since she was half sister to two good horses, Fearless Fox (by Foxlaw), winner of the Goodwood Cup, the Gold Vase at Ascot and second in the St Leger, and Challenge (by Apelle), who won the Jockey Club Stakes and also ran second in the St Leger. She was full sister to a winner, Bold Devil, and half sister to two others, Horchatib and Matona, both by Spion Kop, and to Queen Christina (by Buchan), a beautiful little filly who was trained at Clarehaven during my time, but was not much good on the racecourse, winning two small races in Ireland. However, Queen Christina, who was bought by the Sledmere Stud owned by Sir Richard Sykes, became a fine broodmare, producing nine winners, including the top-class horse Orthodox (by Hyperion), winner of the St James's Palace Stakes, Newmarket Stakes, Free Handicap and other races, and his full sister, Eleanor Cross, a very useful racemare, who also did well at stud.

Molly Adare (by Phalaris), dam of Brazen Molly, did not win but had quite good placed form, while her dam, Molly Desmond (by Desmond), was the best of Pretty Polly's daughters. A winner of the Cheveley Park Stakes, Molly Desmond was beaten a head in the Middle Park Plate, by North Star, and by a similar distance failed to give 8 lb to Gay Crusader, whom Steve Donoghue rated the best horse he ever rode, in the Criterion Stakes.

Thus there was much to recommend Brazen Molly in the racing and breeding records of her immediate ancestors in the tail female line.

Horus, sire of Brazen Molly, was well bred and quite a good racehorse. A half brother to the Two Thousand Guineas winner Flamingo (by Flamboyant), Horus was by the Derby winner Papyrus (Tracery–Miss Matty, by Marcovil) out of Lady Peregrine, by White Eagle (by Gallinule).

Horus, a chesnut with a white blaze, in colour and markings rather like Brigadier Gerard's dam, La Paiva, won the Paradise Stakes at Hurst Park, the King Edward VII Stakes at Ascot and several other races; he also ran third to Trigo and Bosworth in the St Leger. As a boy on holiday from school, I remember seeing Horus beaten a short head for the Tudor Stakes at Sandown by Haste Away (Ellangowan–Quick Thought, by White Eagle), both trained by Jack Jarvis.

The salient point about Brazen Molly's pedigree was that she was inbred 4 × 4 to Gallinule, sire of Pretty Polly.

Probably because she was barren, Brazen Molly, who was submitted by Sir Richard Brooke, did not attract much attention and I was able to get her for 400 guineas. The under bidder was the late Jack (Harvey) Leader, who had a flair for nosing out bargains and always regretted that he had not followed his hunch and gone on bidding. Had he done so I would certainly have lost Brazen Molly, as I had just about reached my limit. Pat Dennis came in with me in her and she went over to Green-mount.

I always had the feeling that the Pretty Polly family would benefit from a tough, foreign outcross, and with this in mind we sent her to Pink Flower, who was by the great German racehorse and sire Oleander, a tail male descendant of Dark Ronald, whose influence has had so beneficial an effect on thoroughbred breeding in Germany.

Pink Flower, a neat, well-made, little bay horse, was bred by Lord Astor and was out of his first-class broodmare Plymstock (Polymelus–Winkipop) who among her many winners bred the Oaks winner, Pennycomequick (by Hurry On).

Pink Flower was a pretty good racehorse. He won the last three of his six races at two years, the Shelford Stakes at three and the Melbourn Handicap at four, both a mile, and was beaten a short head by Kingsway in the Two Thousand Guineas.

Pink Flower had an additional interest for me, as Tom Masson and I had contemplated buying him as a yearling to make a jumper, abandoning the idea because we thought him too small. He was a tough, game little horse, with a nice temperament, but despite his stout pedigree did not stay more than a mile.

Many years later Pink Flower again came into my horizon, when I bought his son Wilwyn, the first winner of the Washington D.C. International, from his owner-breeder Bob Boucher, for Harry Oppenheimer, to stand at his Mauritzfontcin Stud, Kimberley in South Africa, where he has had great success and is still going strong.

Previously I bought an unbroken two-year-old gelding by Pink Flower for £250, from the late Ted Martindale, a fine judge who on retirement from the world of professional polo used to buy backward yearlings as stores; all those I had from him proved winners.

The Pink Flower gelding, who was out of Idle Jest (by Flamboyant), I named Tickled Pink; when applying for the name I found he already had one, Pink Jester, so I paid the fee and changed it. Some people consider it unlucky to change a name, but it certainly was not so in this case as Tickled Pink, trained by George Todd at Manton, won us nine races and ran second in the Goodwood Stakes. In the six 'bumpers' races in which I rode him he was never beaten.

The outcome of the Pink Flower–Brazen Molly mating was an imposing brown colt, whom Ryan Jarvis bought as a yearling and trained to win several races. Named Flower Dust, he was very useful, I would say about 10 lb below the top class. Exported to India, Flower Dust made a great name for himself in that country both as a racehorse and sire.

Brazen Molly threw three further winners, Stokes (by Mieuxcé), Fontanetto (by My Babu) and Cavalry (by Prince Chevalier), who was placed in England and won abroad. Fontanetto had the best pedigree, but possibly on account of his being a double rig★ he was only a moderate racehorse, winning once.

In each case the principle of mating Brazen Molly with a stallion with an outcross, foreign pedigree had been followed, and Stokes proved us right. A big, handsome, impressive brown colt, Stokes was bought by Sir Victor Sassoon as a yearling for 2,000 guineas, chiefly because he owned the sire, Mieuxcé. Stokes proved a bargain, winning the Newmarket Spring Two-Year-Old Stakes, and the Windsor Castle Stakes at Royal Ascot and running second in the Two Thousand Guineas.

Stokes was trained by the late Norman Bertie, former travelling head lad to Fred Darling. Bertie was very easy on his horses, always having them on the big side and never giving them much work. Unfortunately, Stokes was the wrong kind of horse to benefit from this method of training, since apart from his size and strength, he was headstrong and

---

★ A horse in which neither testicle has come down.

obstreperous, requiring a lot of work to keep him in his place. Had he
been under the care of a trainer who believed in giving horses a searching
preparation, Stokes would probably have done better on the racecourse
and might even have won the Two Thousand, instead of finishing second
to Ki Ming.

Despite the mating of Brazen Molly with Prince Chevalier producing
the disappointing Cavalry, a smallish, neat brown colt somewhat lacking
in scope, I felt that we were on the right track, and Pat agreed that we
should send Brazen Molly back to Prince Chevalier, in whom we owned
a share. This we did, two or three years later, the result being La Paiva,
who proved to be Brazen Molly's last foal.

By this time my wife Jean and I had our own stud at East Woodhay
House, where we still live. Though we had owned it for ten years, the land
had been leased by the previous owner, Mr Herbert Pretyman, for that
period to Mr Herbert Blagrave, whose Harwood Stud lay close by, so
that he was able to run the paddocks in conjunction with his own.

La Paiva with Cesarine (by Royal Palace)

Thus we were in the position to start breeding horses on our own land and, at Jean's suggestion, we bought out Pat Dennis's share of La Paiva and changed our policy from breeding to sell to breeding to race.

We had bought East Woodhay House in partnership and ran our stud as such. Though Stokes brought us a good deal of prestige, we made practically nothing out of him. Even if Stokes had made a high price, this would have been subject to taxation and by continuing to breed for sale there was never any hope of hitting the jackpot.

Admittedly, the success of breeding to race was a much more chancy affair, because failure to produce horses able to win good races or command good prices in training, such gains being tax free, would result in financial disaster. But by cutting the number of our mares to a minimum, that is to say two, and taking in a few boarders to help to defray running expenses, the chance seemed worth taking.

Our other mare was Madame Bovary (Linklater–Buck Bean, by Duke of Buckingham–Lady Mere), who was old and had served us well, first by bringing off what for us was a major coup in a selling race and, later, by breeding five winners. So our one hope of making good as owner-breeders lay in La Paiva.

A chesnut, with a blaze and three white socks, La Paiva bore no resemblance whatever to her full brother, Cavalry. Probably, she inherited her colour and markings from her maternal grandsire, Horus, who

La Paiva with her owners at the East Woodhay House Stud

was a chestnut with a blaze, which La Paiva's dam, Brazen Molly, also possessed.

Horus is the only chestnut in the first two removes of La Paiva's pedigree and, although this colour can be carried as a recessive and therefore could come through another source in the pedigree, there is a good chance that it is traceable to Horus. Strength to this theory is added by the fact that the only chestnut in the third remove of La Paiva's pedigree is Lady Peregrine, dam of Horus.

A very well-made mare with particularly good limbs and not easy to fault, La Paiva has more quality and symmetry than had her dam, Brazen Molly, her refinement being attributable to Prince Chevalier, who was distinguished in this respect. Like Prince Chevalier, La Paiva was rather light in the body though deep enough through the girth. Typical of a true lady of quality she has worn well, and those who see her today find it difficult to believe that she was foaled in 1956.

The salient features of La Paiva's pedigree are: she has only one line of Phalaris, sire of her grandam Molly Adare; she has no Gainsborough, Blandford, Hurry On or any notable foreign sire in the first four removes, other than Prince Chevalier; the only duplications in the first five removes are Tracery (4×5), Persimmon (5×5) and Cyllene (5×5), Gallinule appearing twice in the fifth remove, but only in the bottom (Brazen Molly's) half of the pedigree.

Thus, lacking the presence of so many eminent sires, both English-based and foreign, La Paiva offers considerable scope for matings with stallions whose pedigrees contain such sires prominent or duplicated in their pedigree. The closest prepotent sire in La Paiva's pedigree is Phalaris, in the third remove.

La Paiva went to Manton to be trained by George Todd, for whom I used to ride after the war as an amateur on the flat and over hurdles and who, besides Tickled Pink, trained Holy Deadlock (Nomellini–Madame Bovary), who won twelve races for us.

La Paiva was highly strung and not easy to train, being always on the go and rather irritable. I sometimes rode her work and George used to have her led up to the gallops and home again, as she settled better under that system than having her ridden out from the yard. She was usually under the charge of Tom Coffey, an old timer who was formerly at Kingsclere under Evan Williams and 'did' Supreme Court, who also traced to Pretty Polly, coming from the Polly Flinders branch, through Arabella. I sometimes used to ride Supreme Court when he was a backward two-year-old, as I used at that time to ride out with Evan, Kingsclere being conveniently close by.

Supreme Court did not come to himself till the back-end of his two-year-old season, when he won the Horris Hill Stakes at Newbury. Earlier on, no one dreamed he would turn out such a good horse and the best three-year-old of his year, or, doubtless, I would not have been riding him. It is an interesting coincidence that the two best flat race horses I have ever ridden, Brigadier Gerard and Supreme Court, should both trace to Pretty Polly.

Supreme Court was a good ride, but much more immature than Brigadier Gerard, which is understandable since his sire was the Ascot Gold Cup winner Precipitation who, like his sire Hurry On, did not race as a two-year-old. He was a delicate horse who required very little work and but for Evan's fine handling of him, Supreme Court would never have become the brilliant horse he did.

La Paiva's first race was the Elcot Plate for maiden fillies at Newbury on 31 May. There were 22 runners and, ridden by Jimmy Lindley, she finished sixth, beaten just over seven lengths by the winner, Thyra Lee, a fast grey filly by Grey Sovereign and winner later of the Lichfield Nursery at Ascot, the Wantage Nursery at Newbury, carrying 9 st 7 lb, and the Moulton Stakes at Newmarket.

This was quite a promising beginning, concerning which *Raceform* observed 'shaped well'.

La Paiva's next appearance was in the Rosslyn Stakes, six furlongs, at Ascot on 19 July. Lindley was not available to ride as he was at Chepstow. Consequently Lester Piggott was engaged for La Paiva. Whether he did not hear our instructions, or paid no attention to them, he did exactly the opposite. Instead of holding her up until the last two furlongs and not hitting her, he jumped her out of the gate, was in the lead or thereabouts for four furlongs, gave her a couple and then faded from the scene.

In no circumstances do I think she would have won or even finished in the first three, but these tactics were not conducive to getting the best out of her, and having been strictly taught by Victor Gilpin, Tom Masson and George Todd himself, that the first duty of a jockey is to carry out his riding instructions to the letter, I was not very impressed by Piggott's effort; nor was George Todd, who has never had a particularly high regard for jockeys, professional or amateur, and would have preferred to put up one of his own boys. As it was, we were not much wiser than before the race.

La Paiva's final race as a two-year-old was the Queen Bess Maiden Plate, six furlongs, for maiden fillies, at Birmingham. Lindley was in the saddle once more and we thought that she would go pretty well, for her sixteen opponents did not include any of much consequence. She was ridden to orders and at three furlongs appeared to hold a fair chance, but from then on made no progress, finishing seventh or eighth. I was disappointed, as she looked well and had worked nicely at home, and on her previous two runs should have put up a better show. She might have trained off, for by then we were in November, or perhaps she was not too genuine, or just not good enough, which is the reason for the failure of most racehorses.

So La Paiva retired for the winter – that time of hope for owners of flat race horses – to await the outcome of her three-year-old season.

La Paiva did well during the winter, and though still restless and inclined to be irritable, she pleased George when she came to work over a mile and beyond. As the time approached for her first race, the Park Maiden (three-year-old) Handicap, one mile, at Sandown on 16 May, we became quite hopeful that she would end her losing run, since her work at home was very promising. Jimmy Lindley again rode her and she started second favourite at 5 to 1 in a field of sixteen. When she took the lead three furlongs out, it looked as if she was going on to win; but when tackled she just kept plugging on at the same pace, was passed by three others and finished fourth. It was a performance which was difficult to interpret, since she was not devoid of speed nor did she appear to shirk the final battle to the winning post: she just was not good enough, though this did not accord with her work at home.

La Paiva's next race was at Salisbury on 8 July, the Tisbury Maiden Plate, one mile, for three-year-old fillies. She started second favourite in a field of six, the eventual winner Drake's Affair (by Amour Drake), who had previously run second in the Fern Hill Stakes (Handicap) at Ascot, at 6 to 4 on. With Jimmy Lindley riding, La Paiva lay second at the distance, but never threatened to overhaul Drake's Affair, who went on to win by three lengths. Drake's Affair won her next three races, two on successive days at Birmingham.

About this time George Todd noticed that all was not well with La Paiva's near eye; a speck had appeared in it and the vision in it seemed to be affected. In course of time she went quite blind in it and it has now more or less shrivelled up. It seems probable that her sight had begun to deteriorate some time earlier, and that in consequence she was nervous when she approached the front in a race, though at home where she knew the gallops and the other horses it did not make the same difference. This would account for her disappointing form on the racecourse as compared with some of the good gallops she put up at home.

La Paiva had only two more races, the Newtown Stakes, one and a half miles, for maiden three-year-olds, at Newbury, and the Manton Maiden Plate, one and a quarter miles, at Newbury. In the former she finished fourth, ridden by Jimmy Lindley, who by now must have been getting rather tired of her, and in the latter fifth, this time ridden by John Friar, one of George Todd's apprentices, claiming 7 lb.

La Paiva then came back to us, preparatory to going to stud in 1960.

4 *La Paiva goes to Stud*

It has always seemed wise to me to start a mare's career at stud by sending her to a fast horse, who gets, or seems likely to get, two-year-old winners. In this way the breeder stands a good chance of appraising her future merit as a broodmare fairly quickly, as opposed to mating her with a sire whose stock do not come to hand as two-year-olds. On this principle, in her first season La Paiva went to Gratitude.

Gratitude was an unproved sire, because he had not yet had a runner, but it seemed reasonable to believe that he might sire two-year-old winners. To start with, he was a fast, good racehorse, who at two years won the New Stakes at Ascot, at three the Queensbury Handicap at Newmarket and at four the Micklegate Handicap at York, carrying 9 st 7 lb, and the Nunthorpe Stakes, all over five furlongs. Besides, he had a very fast pedigree, being by the sprinter Golden Cloud (by Gold Bridge) out of Verdura, by Court Martial. In tail female line of descent he went back to Miranda, a full sister to Pretty Polly.

A big, fine-looking, powerful chesnut horse, Gratitude had a beautiful temperament and was a sound, tough and genuine horse. He was bred and raced by the late Major L. B. Holliday and trained by Humphrey Cottrill; and at the end of his racing career was bought in partnership by Teddy Lambton and the late Nicky Morriss, owner of the Banstead Manor Stud near Newmarket.

Gratitude, who stood at the Hon. Mrs George Lambton's Phantom Stud at Newmarket, where Golden Cloud's sire, Gold Bridge, used to stand, commanded the modest fee of £148, which from our point of view was an added attraction.

On paper it looked a good enough mating, since Gratitude supplied the important influences of Orby, Blandford and Hurry On, all absent in La Paiva, and a duplication of Phalaris, the closest prepotent influence in La Paiva's pedigree.

La Paiva got in foal and on 22 March 1961, produced a fine chesnut colt, which we named The Travellers', after the Travellers' Club in Paris, once the home of the original La Paiva, a famous courtesan who is portrayed in bas relief, in the nude, in the building.

The Travellers' was an imposing colt, very like Gratitude but taller, with more daylight under him. We offered him to George Todd to train, when he was a yearling, but he turned him down, as he had made up his mind to take no yearlings that season and even refused at first a grey colt by Buisson Ardent belonging to an old patron, Tommy Frost, but relented only when Tommy agreed to have him broken by Scotty Pringle at Newmarket and then sent to Manton later. It was as well that George changed his mind over the grey colt, as he turned out to be Roan Rocket, who won five races including the St James's Palace Stakes, Sussex Stakes and Rous Memorial Stakes, Goodwood, and was beaten a short head by Canisbay in the Eclipse Stakes.

So we sent The Travellers' to Tom Masson at Lewes, with whom we had trained when we lived in Sussex, only changing to George Todd when we moved to East Woodhay, because Lewes was so far away.

The Travellers' made his first appearance at Kempton in the spring, showing speed but fading out of the picture before the finish. He had grown and, at the time, Jean remarked that he looked more like a horse who should be put by as a store than one to be exploited as a two-year-old. But I was very keen to try to make him a winner, for the sake of La Paiva's reputation as a broodmare, so I compromised by putting him by till the autumn, when he had three more races. In the last of these, the Theale Maiden Plate at Newbury, he finished a respectable fifth in a biggish field and there seemed hope that he might prove relatively better as a three-year-old. But the following season he was just as backward and in his three races ran deplorably, except that he always showed a measure of speed. We then had him home, gelded him and I looked round for a possible buyer for him as a prospective jumper, without success. Meanwhile, he thrived, grew stronger and seemed to develop more confidence in himself.

One day I was in my office at *The British Racehorse* in Clarges Street, when a gentleman called to see me. He introduced himself as Mr Shrive, told me that he had been a subscriber to *The British Racehorse* since it began, that he owned a small S. P. business in Leicester and thought he would like to buy a racehorse, on which matter he had come to seek my advice. He was prepared to spend up to £3,000 or so and asked me if I would try to find him one. I agreed to do so and, when he asked me about a suitable trainer, advised him to choose one with a fairly small stable in the Midlands or North, suggesting Joe Hartigan at Middleham.

After he had gone, it suddenly occurred to me that Mr Shrive's best plan would be to lease a horse with the option of purchase. In this case, if the horse did not come up to expectations, he could return him and still have the money he proposed to spend. If the horse pleased him, he could exercise his option to buy him. While trying to think of a suitable horse, it suddenly occurred to me that The Travellers' might fit the bill. I put this idea to Mr Shrive and to Joe Hartigan, who had agreed to train the horse if we found one, and they thought it a good one, so The Travellers' was sent to Joe at Middleham.

It proved a successful arrangement, as The Travellers' won four races for Mr Shrive, who took up his option to buy him not long after he won for the first time. His victories were not of a very high order and ranged from seven to eleven furlongs, but one was especially pleasing to Mr Shrive, since it was gained at his home meeting, Leicester, when he took a party of friends and clients to see The Travellers' run, his rider being Lester Piggott. After his fourth success The Travellers' never won again and was sold after running unplaced two or three times, having made La Paiva the dam of a winner and given his purchaser a good run for his money. Little did any of us think at the time that The Travellers' was destined to become a half brother to one of the greatest horses ever to appear on the Turf.

In 1961 La Paiva again visited Gratitude, but was barren to him. In fact, for her first seven seasons at stud La Paiva was an every other year breeder, the sequence being broken when she foaled Brigadier Gerard the year after she produced Town Major (by Major Portion).

When in 1962 La Paiva visited Donore, The Travellers' had not won, the mare was not in foal and, altogether, the outlook was rather bleak. Thus we were not in a position to choose an expensive sire and in this respect, Donore, whose stud fee was £98, fitted the bill well.

An attractive grey horse, Donore (Fair Trial–Zobeida, by Dastur) had proved a good, consistent racehorse who ran for five seasons, showed excellent form throughout and retired sound. His most important victory was in the Wokingham Stakes as a four-year-old, and he ran second in the race when he was six, to the subsequent Cambridgeshire winner Jupiter; but the best performances he put up were probably when he ran second to Palestine (Fair Trial–Una, by Tetratema) in the Champagne Stakes at Doncaster and the Henry VIII Stakes at Hurst Park. Palestine was a brilliant horse up to a mile, his victories also including the Coventry Stakes, National Breeders Stakes, Gimcrack Stakes, the Two Thousand

Guineas, St James's Palace Stakes and Sussex Stakes.

Owned first by Sir Humphrey de Trafford and afterwards by Lord Rosebery, Donore stood at the Mentmore Stud and got his fair share of winners, including Lord Rosebery's good filly Donna, who bred an even better one in Gwen (by Abernant), as well as several other horses of merit.

The Donore–La Paiva mating looked promising on paper: the aspect of conformation held water, as did that of temperament, soundness and racing performance; and so far as breeding was concerned Donore supplied a number of important influences not present in La Paiva, notably Fair Trial, Solario, The Tetrarch and Sunstar, the only duplication of a significant name being that of Phalaris, paternal great-grandsire of Donore and sire of La Paiva's grandam Molly Adare.

In due course La Paiva foaled a good, strong, well-made chesnut colt, who bore little resemblance to Donore but was rather like La Paiva's maternal grandsire, Horus. As with both Horus and La Paiva, the colt – whom I named Delaunay (the first actor manager of the Comédie Française) – had a blaze and a certain amount of white about his legs.

When Delaunay was a yearling, our financial situation was such that we felt that, instead of keeping to our policy of putting all our home-bred horses in training, Delaunay and his companion, a brown colt by March Past out of Madame Bovary, called Macmahon after Napoleon's general – his subsequent owner changed his name to March Storm – would have to go up for sale. It proved an error of judgment.

Delaunay made 700 guineas and the March Past colt 720 guineas. The buyer of Delaunay was Jack Jarvis, bidding on behalf of Lord Rosebery, and it was no consolation to learn afterwards that Jack was empowered to go to a great deal more for him, had it been necessary.

Delaunay proved a good servant to his new owner. He won the last running of the Arundel Castle Private Sweepstakes, for two-year-olds at Goodwood, and a race at Nottingham in his first season. At three he was successful in two good handicaps, at Newmarket and Lingfield; he also won for Lord Rosebery as a four-year-old and was then sold, but continued to win in less distinguished company, was placed over hurdles and finally was retired to stud. The March Past colt also won, both on the flat and over jumps. Had we put the pair in training and then sold them, we would have been far better off.

When in training, Delaunay threw out a very pronounced curb, but this later subsided and did not appear to affect his performance. When La Paiva's next two progeny also threw out curbs, I realised that this factor must be carried by her as a recessive.

In 1964 La Paiva went to Rockefella, who was by Hyperion out of Rockfel, a really good mare who won the One Thousand Guineas, Oaks and Champion Stakes, in which she beat Pasch (Blandford–Pasca, by Manna), winner of the Two Thousand Guineas and the Eclipse Stakes. Unfortunately Rockfel died after she produced Rockefella.

Trained by Ossie Bell at Lambourn, Rockefella, who was foaled in 1941, ran second at Ascot from two starts as a two-year-old and in the next season won three races and was once unplaced. His merit as a racehorse was difficult to assess since he coughed for most of his three-year-old season, as a result of which his victories all occurred between 14 October and 4 November, so he missed the classics and met no outstanding horses.

A brown horse, 16.1 in height, Rockefella had something in him of both his sire Hyperion and his maternal grandsire, Felstead. He was more on the leg than Hyperion, but had the latter's head and his hocks were a little bent, whereas Hyperion's were perfect.

Though an old horse in 1964, Rockefella had retained his vitality and proved a successful sire, his stock including the Two Thousand Guineas winner Rockavon, those notable brothers Gay Time, Elopement and Cash and Courage, Rich and Rare, a brilliant two-year-old who belonged to Tom Blackwell, a friend of many years, Castle Rock, a good horse belonging to Lord Rosebery, and the Cambridgeshire winner Richer. At 300 guineas Rockefella was not dear, despite his age, since he was a good foal getter.

Some breeders are prejudiced against old stallions, often wrongly. Provided his health is unimpaired and his fertility is still good, a stallion is just as likely to get a good horse at twenty as at six. In fact, some have sired their best offspring in their last season at stud, for instance Donatello II, whose best son, Crepello, was among his sire's last crop.

On 9 March 1965, La Paiva foaled a bay colt, who bore a considerable resemblance to Rockefella, except that he had a small, narrow star and snip on his nose and four white socks. His hocks were rather bent and both had curbs, so he could not be said to be good looking, but he was strong, tough and active and looked as if he would race.

I had a two-year-old, Bell Crofts (Arctic Time–Mrs Dale) with Dick Hern whose stable at that time was owned by Jakie Astor, an old friend with whom I had served in Phantom and the S.A.S. during the war. So the Rockefella yearling, whom we named General Wolfe, went to join Bell Crofts.

Bell Crofts, whom I bought as a yearling for 750 guineas at Newmarket, a nice-looking grey, won as a three-year-old and her first foal, Eleanor Bold (by Queen's Hussar) won as a two-year-old in 1972.

General Wolfe shaped well in his spring work at West Ilsley and twice went rather better than a nice-looking grey colt belonging to Jakie Astor, called Loveridge (Grey Sovereign–Sally Loveridge, by Nearco). He made his first appearance in the Lansdown Stakes, five furlongs, at Bath on 24 May. He was ridden by one of the stable work-jockeys, Reg Cartwright, as Joe Mercer had the chance to ride the probable winner, Tramperlane, who was odds on. Though he started at 20 to 1, I was expecting him to run well, since the quality of the horses with whom he had been working was rather better than is found generally in a minor race at Bath. This was not to be. As soon as he came into the paddock, General Wolfe began to neigh at the top of his voice, cast lecherous glances at every filly in sight and became thoroughly upset. In the race, he showed not the slightest inclination to exert himself and finished a moderate fifth of seven, the race being won by the second favourite, Intimidation, trained by Ginger Dennistoun, an old friend from Sandhurst days; a head away in second place came the favourite, Tramperlane.

It was a deplorable effort and the immediate reaction of Dick Hern and myself was to get rid of him at the first available sale, a decision which Jean rightly condemned as unduly precipitate and upon which Deirdre Sutton, who was standing with us during the discussion, observed, 'that's how people get bargains'.

It is always a mistake to write off a horse on his first run, just as it is unwise to keep on making excuses for continued failure. So bearing in mind Atty Corbett's remark about one of his owners, 'with him there's nothing between Ascot and Ascot Sales', we decided to give General Wolfe another chance.

General Wolfe's next race was at Nottingham on 5 June. This time he was ridden by Joe Mercer,* which was the first occasion upon which he had ridden one of La Paiva's offspring. The experience can have given him little inkling of his future partnership with a half brother of such immeasurably greater superiority as Brigadier Gerard.

Fitted with blinkers, General Wolfe ran fast for two or three furlongs and then faded out of the picture. While the narrower field of vision afforded him by the blinkers prevented him looking about to the same extent as he had done at Bath, it was clear that his mind was not on racing and that if his thoughts continued in this vein, which seemed sure to

---

* One of the best and most stylish riders of the postwar era, Joe learned his profession in that most spartan of schools, the late Major Sneyd's establishment, from which also emanated those fine jockeys Eph and Doug Smith.

happen, he would be useless as a racehorse. Thus two alternatives remained, to get rid of him, or to geld him in the hope that the spirit of competition would replace thoughts of eroticism. We decided upon the latter path and he returned to our stud, was operated on and in due course went back into training with Dick Hern.

There had never been much wrong with General Wolfe's behaviour on the training ground, so the success or failure of having him gelded could not be determined until he raced. He had lost no condition through being gelded – being an active, slightly irritable horse, always on the go, he had not been in any way gross as an entire – and thrived on his work.

The occasion for arriving at the moment of truth was the Potential Stayers' Stakes, six furlongs, at Windsor on 7 October. General Wolfe was ridden by Wally Swinburn, whom I first knew as an apprentice to Sam Armstrong when I was riding regularly for Sam in amateur races. A good rider, now successfully operating in France, Wally's victories of note at that time included the Irish One Thousand Guineas of 1972 on Pidget (Fortino II–Primlace, by Chamossaire). There were fifteen runners, and General Wolfe ran a fine race to finish fourth, the most satisfactory part of his performance in general being that he behaved impeccably and kept his mind on racing.

Some time afterwards, the late Ronnie Basset asked me to find him a horse which would give him some fun without costing too much money. I looked around without success and was beginning to lose hope of finding anything when it suddenly occurred to me that General Wolfe might suit him. He was a maiden, so was easy to place; having had three runs without finishing in the first three, he was certain to be reasonably handicapped; he was sure to improve, as he had not been hard trained after being gelded, yet had run creditably; and he was bred to stay at least a mile and a quarter.

I put the idea up to Ronnie and he immediately decided that he would like to have the horse and agreed to leave him with Dick Hern, which was a contingency of the sale. It proved a happy transaction, for General Wolfe won six races and broke the record for one and a half miles at Lingfield. He then began to break blood vessels, so was found a good home as a hack in France, where he is now distinguishing himself in dressage competitions.

Ronnie had become very fond of General Wolfe, and I was greatly touched that when he went into hospital before he died he insisted on taking with him a silver statuette which the General had won.

The success of General Wolfe was heartening because he had proved himself markedly better than The Travellers' and indicated that his dam possessed the aptitude for producing winners to two stallions of widely differing types. With mares such as her, it is a matter of striking the right mating and a good horse will quite likely result. So far, I had failed to hit the bull's-eye.

True to form, La Paiva was barren to her next covering, by Pandofell (Solar Slipper–Nadika, by Nosca), a tough versatile horse, who had won from ten furlongs to the two and a half miles of the Ascot Gold Cup.

In 1966 La Paiva went to Major Portion (Court Martial–Better Half, by Mieuxcé), a very good racehorse up to a mile, winning six races, including the Middle Park Stakes, the St James's Palace Stakes, the Queen Elizabeth II Stakes and the Chesham Stakes. His only defeats in eight races were in the Two Thousand Guineas, in which he was beaten half a length by Pall Mall, and the Champion Stakes, when he finished third, the race being won by the brilliant Bella Paola, winner also of the One Thousand Guineas and the Oaks. Though he has sired his fair share of winners, Major Portion has been rather a disappointing sire; his only classic winner is Soleil, who won the French Two Thousand Guineas.

On 17 February 1967, La Paiva foaled an attractive colt to Major Portion. He was a chesnut with a hint of red in his coat, and a white blaze, in general with a strong look of Major Portion. He had a nice nature and was strong, active and intelligent, but excitable. He went into training with Dick Hern at the time when the stable was paralysed with a virus, but came through with no ill effects. His chief trouble was that, like many horses of the male line of Court Martial (sire of Major Portion), he was no good on firm ground and, if raced on it was liable to get sore shins or become jarred.

The aspect of ability to gallop on a certain type of going or not, is seldom given thought by breeders, but experience has taught me that it is important and should not be left out of calculations.

Practically no horse is equally good on any kind of ground, but some are more adaptable than others; they may not be able to show their best form in soft or on hard ground, but they are capable of running reasonably well, as opposed to being tailed off. Though Brigadier Gerard was at least a stone better on firm ground than in heavy going, he could still beat good horses under conditions highly unsuitable to him, as he proved in the St James's Palace Stakes and the Champion Stakes in 1971.

A fault in the Major Portion–La Paiva mating was that it brought together two influences for inability to gallop freely on firm ground, Major Portion and La Paiva's sire Prince Chevalier, whose close proximity in his pedigree with Mieuxcé produced a combination of two excitable elements.

Having recovered from sore shins in the spring, Town Major worked well enough to suggest that he had at least a measure of ability. But the stable was completely in the dark as to the merit of its horses, consequent to the virus, and though we were nearly at the end of May, it had hardly had a runner and no winner. In fact, when Town Major appeared for the Portsmouth Road Plate at Sandown on 27 May, I am not at all sure that he was not the stable's first runner after the scourge.

At home, Town Major's excitability soon made itself evident: he could not bear cantering in the string, fly-jumping in an endeavour to get to the front. When on his own and ridden by someone in whom he had confidence, he went well, as he did at West Ilsley for Harry Grant, an old-timer who is a good and quiet rider.

After being saddled, he kept kicking as he walked down towards the parade ring, a habit which never left him during his racing career, and when loosed on reaching the course he gave a couple of fly jumps and went down to the post as if propelled by a rocket. One or two people backed him light-heartedly because of this spectacular display. But neither Dick Hern nor I were imbued with such optimism; we stood at the corner of the stands at the winning-post end, together with Jakie Astor and Brook Holliday, wondering how he would perform, they almost as much concerned as I, since he was, as it were, a scout for the other two-year-olds in the stable.

Though of an entirely different nature, Town Major's running was hardly less spectacular than that of his ancestress Pretty Polly over the identical course. Of the seventeen runners, he was almost last leaving the stalls. At half way he was some thirty lengths behind the leaders, and although he had improved his position as the leaders entered the last furlong, his chance of winning appeared utterly hopeless. But suddenly he began to make up ground and, literally, to fly past his opponents. So effective was his final run that at the winning post he had half a length to spare over the second horse, Bourbon Street, with the favourite, Round the Moon, a further three-quarters of a length away in third place. Not surprisingly, Town Major started at 100 to 6, paying the remarkable price of 191s 8d on the Tote.

I was speechless with astonishment and delight, for the performance promised well, since Bourbon Street was a previous winner and Round the Moon had clearly shown ability at home, to make him favourite.

Joe Mercer reported that Town Major had not found his action until the last two furlongs, but was inclined to think that his success might have been a fluke, as a result of the leaders expending their energy against each other during the early part of the race. I was more optimistic and decided to run Town Major in the Coventry Stakes at Royal Ascot, to determine his true ability, one way or the other.

He ran quite a good race, being narrowly beaten for fourth place, behind Prince Tenderfoot (Blue Prince–La Tendresse, by Grey Sovereign), who won comfortably. Though the going was described as good, it was firmer than Town Major liked and he was sore after the race. He never fulfilled his early promise and his spectacular debut was his only victory, though he was placed as a three-year-old, giving the subsequent Ayr Gold Cup winner John Splendid 9 lb, and in France as a four-year-old, eventually being sold to go to Australia as a stallion.

He was an unlucky horse: it took him over a year to recover properly from being jarred as a two-year-old; he was badly knocked about on the journey to France and no sooner had he come right than he injured himself through getting cast in his box. Added to this, he threw out a curb while in training. I shall always believe that Town Major was considerably better than his overall record shows.

The lesson of Town Major was that we still had not found the right mating for La Paiva. In this case the mistake may have lain in the bringing together, close up in the pedigree, of the excitable influences of Mieuxcé and Prince Chevalier, both tail male descendants of St Simon. Weight is added to this theory by the fact that, when tried again, it resulted in the useful but volatile Brigade Major, who also shares with Town Major the complete inability to gallop on firm ground.

5 *Planning the Birth of the Brigadier*

Town Major had not appeared on the scene when the time came for the 1967 mating of La Paiva to be arranged, so the data he provided later was not available.

The points to be considered were: First, a sire who, so far as it was possible to discern, did not have the factor for curbs, since this fault had appeared in Delaunay and General Wolfe. Second, to choose a sire likely to produce a two-year-old winner who, at the same time, had reasonable prospects of training on and getting a mile, as the racing horizon of a pure sprinter is restricted, especially after a horse's three-year-old season, while a horse with no prospect of winning before he was three would represent a long and expensive wait before the chance of any return. Third, that the pedigree of the stallion offered a suitable blend with that of La Paiva. Fourth, that the stallion should be sound, tough, courageous and well made. And, finally, that his fee should be within my pocket.

Since, from the practical aspect, the last clause was the most important, I began by going through the list of stallions standing at a modest fee. The one who attracted my interest most was Queen's Hussar. He stood at £250 and at that time few breeders appeared to want his services, for according to the records of the previous season he had only covered fifteen mares, which included those from the Highclere Stud of his owner, Lord Carnarvon.

Queen's Hussar is lucky to be in existence. His sire March Past, who was bred in 1950 by the late Captain 'Inky' Ingram, was bought as a yearling by his future trainer, Ken Cundell, for 770 guineas at the Doncaster Yearling Sales, on behalf of Mrs G. Trimmer-Thompson, and was the first horse she ever owned. He was a big, plain, backward yearling, coal black, and gave the impression that he would take some time to come to hand. Therefore Ken Cundell thought that it might be wise to geld him, which he considered advising Mrs Trimmer-Thompson to have done. However, as March Past was her first racehorse and the apple of her eye,

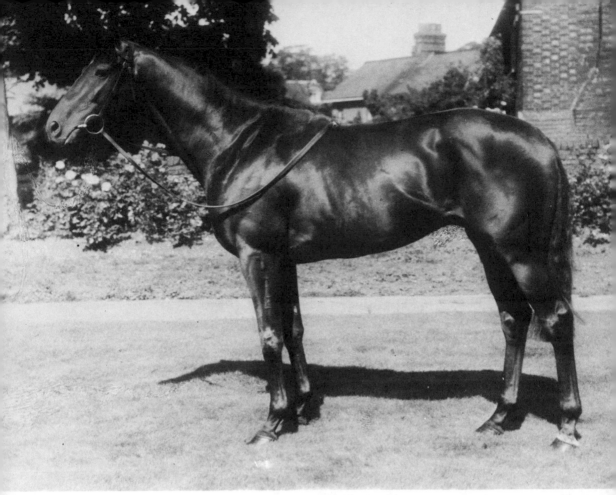

Queen's Hussar

he came to the conclusion that the suggestion might upset her, so decided to shelve the idea and see how March Past progressed. Had the plan to geld March Past been followed up, there would have been no Queen's Hussar and no Brigadier Gerard.

In the spring of his two-year-old season March Past showed little sign of future promise, but as summer approached he began to improve. He was still backward when he appeared for the first time on a racecourse, on 25 June at Newbury, in the Berkshire Stakes, which was to be the first race contested and won by Brigadier Gerard. March Past, ridden by Lester Piggott, failed to finish in the first six, but *Raceform* noted him as 'nice colt, backward'.

The following month, at Salisbury, March Past, still backward, ran a moderate third of five in the Hurstbourne Stakes, again ridden by Lester Piggott and starting at 25 to 1. Fourth of seventeen at Bath a week later, March Past then found form, winning his remaining four starts that season, the Vauxhall Stakes at Kempton, the High Hill Nursery at Bath, the Doncaster Produce Stakes and the Solario Stakes at Sandown, the last two being races of considerable standing; in all these victories he was partnered by Lester Piggott.

March Past raced for two more seasons, proving himself a good, consistent, courageous horse from six furlongs to a mile. His most important victories were the Greenham Stakes at Newbury, the Red Rose Stakes at Manchester, the Wokingham Stakes at Royal Ascot, which he won as a four-year-old carrying equal top weight of 9 stone, and the Scarbrough Stakes at Doncaster.

At that time Ken Cundell trained also for Mr George Stephens, who both bred and raced horses. Among his mares was a grey named Jojo, by Vilmorin (Gold Bridge–Queen of the Meadows, by Fairway) out of Fairy Jane, by Fair Trial (by Fairway) and thus inbred to Fairway 3 × 3.

At Ken's suggestion, George Stephens sent Jojo to March Past two years running. The first mating produced Scots Fusilier, who was gelded and for his owner-trainer, Atty Corbett, won innumerable races from five furlongs to one and a quarter miles and at his peak was a good handicapper.

The next foal was Queen's Hussar.

Queen's Hussar is a particularly well-made individual. Like Fairway, to whom he is inbred 4 × 4 × 4, he never carried much flesh, but was an almost perfect equine racing machine, with the most beautiful, clean, sound limbs one could wish to see on a horse. In fact, he had better forelegs than Fairway, who like many of the progeny of Phalaris was somewhat back at the knee. What, from my point of view, was even more important was that he had a perfect hind leg, without a trace of curbs. Nor, so far as I could detect, did Queen's Hussar's pedigree suggest any factor for curbs or bad hocks.

The 3 × 3 inbreeding to Fair Trial, which his pedigree shows, indicated the possibility of any offspring of Queen's Hussar turning a foot out and being unable to give his best running on firm ground. So far as I can recall, Queen's Hussar is perfectly straight in his action and, despite the proximity of the two lines of Fair Trial, both he and his offspring have a distinct preference for firm, as opposed to soft, going. The latter trait is counterbalanced by La Paiva, since virtually all horses by her sire, Prince Chevalier, go well in soft going. The effect of these two opposing traits in Brigadier Gerard is interesting. Though at his best on firm ground, he was by no means incapable of dealing with soft going.

The feature of Queen's Hussar, in relation to his pedigree, which interested me most was that he bore no resemblance to his sire, March

Past, to his dam, Jojo, to her sire, Vilmorin, or to Fair Trial, to whom he is inbred. But there was a distinct look of Fairway about him in his racing-like build, quality – much more marked than in his parents or grand-parents – and the activity and nervous energy which is so distinctive an inheritance from the great St Simon, to whom Fairway is inbred 3×4. Apart from the six lines of St Simon introduced through the three lines of Fairway, Queen's Hussar had several others further back in his pedigree, one notable line being through March Past's maternal grandsire, William of Valence, a tail male descendant of St Simon, through Chaucer, Prince Chimay and Vatout, sire of William of Valence.

William of Valence, a free-sweating, excitable horse, and Stratford (sire of March Past's grandam Permavon), a short-running influence and sire of a number of horses whose character left something to be desired, are two names I would not grieve to see absent in a pedigree; but fortun-ately their racing ability and not their undesirable qualities appear to have emerged in March Past and Queen's Hussar. As regards temperament, Fair Trial is a good influence in any pedigree and the fact that Queen's Hussar is inbred to him may well have counterbalanced the unhappier side of William of Valence and Stratford. At any rate, Queen's Hussar, though full of nervous energy and not the acme of docility, was a courageous, genuine horse, while Brigadier Gerard has a perfect temperament.

Scots Fusilier having served him so well, Atty Corbett approached his breeder, George Stephens, on the matter of buying the full brother, then a yearling. Stephens said that he would take £1,000 for him and at this price the colt passed into Atty's ownership and in due course arrived at his yard in Compton, Berkshire, where he trained before moving to Newmarket.

It is an odd coincidence, which Ken Cundell pointed out to me, that Brigadier Gerard, Queen's Hussar and March Past were all trained in the area round Newbury, while Mill Reef, second to Brigadier Gerard in the Two Thousand Guineas and his great rival in public esteem, was under the care of Ian Balding at Kingsclere, also just outside Newbury.

Not long after Atty Corbett acquired the March Past–Jojo colt, his accountant informed him that if he bought horses and raced them himself he would go broke, advising him to find a buyer for the colt from among his patrons. These, at that time, included Lord Carnarvon, to whom the colt was offered at cost price. Lord Carnarvon intimated that he would prefer to take a half share with Atty, but this was not the accountant's idea of how his client should do business, so Lord Carnarvon agreed to take the colt over altogether.

He named him Queen's Hussar, after his regiment. There is a saying on the Turf that a good horse never has a bad name and, in this respect, Queen's Hussar certainly was given a propitious start in his racing life. Having cost only £1,000 and being unfashionably bred, Queen's Hussar was given no classic engagements.

The first time he was galloped, Queen's Hussar showed that he had real ability. Atty Corbett considers him by far the best horse he has ever trained and relates that, like Brigadier Gerard, he never put up a bad gallop in his life.

Because a horse is unfashionably bred and has not cost much, it does not follow that he may not be a good one and, if this is apparent in his work, his career should be planned according to his ability and not his background. But only too often a horse is treated by the measure of what he is expected to be, rather than what he is. Thus well-bred and/or expensive horses of little merit sometimes have their careers mapped out on classic lines, while good but unfashionably bred and/or cheap horses tend to be raced in the light of their price and pedigree.

In some hands, Brigadier Gerard, who like Queen's Hussar showed brilliance in March, would have been exploited as a two-year-old, given no time to develop and, in consequence, never have achieved all he did. Queen's Hussar was less fortunate and has always given me the impression that under a more restrained policy he would have made an appreciably greater name for himself than was the case.

As it was, his owner decided that his first main objective was to be the Cuddington Stakes at the Epsom Spring Meeting and that, since it is the exception rather than the rule for horses to win at Epsom without a previous race, he should have a preliminary outing in the Cannon Yard Plate at Windsor on 6 April. By contrast, Brigadier Gerard's first appearance was on 23 June, in the Berkshire Stakes at Newbury.

Starting at 9 to 4 on, Queen's Hussar won his Windsor race by six lengths, going on to take the Cuddington Stakes by five lengths at the more lucrative price of 11 to 10 against; in both races he was ridden by Lester Piggott.

Before his next race, the Windsor Castle Stakes at Royal Ascot, Queen's Hussar hit himself and, as a result, was not at his best, having missed a gallop or two. Nevertheless he ran second to a fast two-year-old, Summer Day (Golden Cloud–Sweet Resolve, by Honeyway), trained for the late Major Henry Broughton (afterwards Lord Fairhaven) by Jack Waugh at Newmarket and ridden by the late Eph Smith.

Another second followed in the Berkshire Stakes at Newbury when, ridden by Joe Mercer, Queen's Hussar failed by half a length to give 7 lb to Akbar (King of the Tudors–Machan, by Big Game), owned by John Aspinall, better known for his wild animals than his racehorses, and trained by Bernard van Cutsem, Eph Smith again being the successful jockey.

Queen's Hussar was not kept idle, for he came out a fortnight later at Salisbury to finish third behind Forearmed (Premonition–Armentières, by Hyperion), to whom he was attempting to give a stone, and Emerald Cross, for the Champagne Stakes, ridden by Joe Mercer. Another defeat came at Goodwood, in the Findon Stakes won by Daybreak (Golden Cloud–Julie, by Denturius), a very fast colt, closely inbred to Gold Bridge. Queen's Hussar finished third, receiving 6 lb from Daybreak, who won by four lengths, Irish Sky separating the pair.

Lord Carnarvon has always conducted his racing policy on the principle that 'it is better to sell and regret than keep and regret', a precept which has a measure of prudence behind it but can be a two-edged sword, as his lordship himself experienced when selling the subsequent Derby winner Blenheim as a yearling, his half brother King Salmon before he won the Coronation Cup and the Eclipse Stakes, as well as a full brother to Blenheim named His Grace, who won for his fortunate buyer, the late Mr J. V. Rank, more than he gave for him.

Despite these unhappy experiences, after Queen's Hussar's four successive failures his owner expressed a desire to get out of him, only the pressure from his son and his trainer causing him to change his mind.

When he next ran, in the Washington Singer Stakes at Newbury, a race won later by Brigadier Gerard, Queen's Hussar wore blinkers as, according to his owner, Joe Mercer had remarked that Queen's Hussar looked about him when he had ridden him and suggested that blinkers might prevent him from doing so.

This time he was ridden by Scobie Breasley and, making all the running, he won by ten lengths from Merchant Venturer (Hornbeam–Martinhoe, by Mieuxcé), who was having his first race and the following year ran second to Relko in the Derby. Whether this impressive performance can be attributed to the addition of blinkers, or not, is a matter of opinion, as he had won twice without them. Atty Corbett avers that he always went best for Breasley, so both factors may have played their part. At any rate he always wore them afterwards, though he never showed any sign of being anything but an honest and courageous racehorse.

Queen's Hussar returned to Newbury a month later for the Highclere

Nursery, in which he carried 9 st 7 lb, and finished a creditable fifth, ridden by Lester Piggott, being three lengths and a head behind the winner, Seymour (High Treason–Admiral's Frolic, by Admiral's Walk), whose owner, Miss P. Major, has the distinction of being a former Head Girl at Heathfield; Queen's Hussar was trying to give the winner 24 lb.

His final race of the season, his ninth – Brigadier Gerard ran only four times as a two-year-old – was the Rous Memorial Stakes at Newmarket. Ridden by Breasley and carrying 9 st 6 lb, he made all the running to win by five lengths, giving the second, Hong Kong, a stone and starting third favourite at 100 to 30. It says much for Queen's Hussar that he began the season with a victory on 6 April and ended the same way on 16 October.

In his second season Queen's Hussar again started nine times, against Brigadier Gerard's six. He began by running fifth in the Two Thousand Guineas Trial at Kempton on 13 April, then third on 6 May in the Palace House Stakes, five furlongs, won easily by Sammy Davis (Whistler–Samaria, by Migoli) from Polybius. In both races he was ridden by Breasley and the going was softer than he liked. He then won the Lockinge Stakes, one mile, by a short head and three-quarters of a length from two good milers, Cyrus and Romulus. This was the race in which Brigadier Gerard made his first appearance as a four-year-old.

A third to The Creditor (Crepello–The Accused, by Fair Trial) and Brief Flight in the Jersey Stakes, seven furlongs, at Royal Ascot, on ground disadvantageously soft for him, was followed by a fourth in the July Cup, won by Mr Paul Mellon's top-class grey filly Secret Step (Native Dancer–Tap Day, by Bull Lea), trained by the late Peter Hastings-Bass, another brilliant filly, Matatina, finishing second.

Then came the most important success of Queen's Hussar's career, the Sussex Stakes at Goodwood, which he won by a head from the Irish Two Thousand Guineas winner Linacre, sire of Perdu, whom Atty Corbett trained to win the Coventry Stakes at Royal Ascot and the July Stakes at Newmarket in 1972. In both the Sussex Stakes and the July Cup, Queen's Hussar was ridden by Ron Hutchinson.

This was Queen's Hussar's last victory as a three-year-old. Again ridden by Hutchinson, he was beaten a head in the Hungerford Stakes at Newbury in very heavy going by Dunce Cap (Tom Fool–Bright Cap, by Bull Lea), a charming filly owned by Mr Jock Whitney, a former U.S. Ambassador to England and famous as the owner of that pre-war chasing star of the first magnitude, Easter Hero.

When sent to Newmarket for the Invicta Stakes, Queen's Hussar again found the going softer than he liked so that it is not surprising that he could finish only third to the brilliant filly The Creditor, from Noel Murless's stable, another good filly Fair Astronomer, dividing the pair. His final race of 1963 was the Prix Perth, one mile, at Saint-Cloud, in which he was unplaced.

As a four-year-old, Queen's Hussar ran only three times. He carried top weight of 10 st in the Gnome Cup, seven furlongs, at Newbury, in which he was fifth, ran unplaced with equal top weight of 9 st 11 lb in the Victoria Cup won by Blazing Scent (Blason–Frigid Flower, by Arctic Prince), trained by George Todd and carrying 7 st 11 lb, on dead going, and finally gained a bloodless victory in the Cavendish Stakes at Sandown worth £787½, one mile, against his single opponent, the three-year-old Cumshaw, whom he beat by twelve lengths. His trainer, Atty Corbett, told me that at this point Queen's Hussar was better than he had ever been in his life; he looked magnificent, was as sound as a bell, could have won other good races and, he felt sure, would have stayed one and a quarter miles, which his full brother, Scots Fusilier, proved able to do. In his four-year-old season, Brigadier Gerard ran eight times, and since most of the stock of Queen's Hussar seem to improve with age it is reasonable to suppose that he conformed to the same pattern.

However, Queen's Hussar's owner decided to retire him, a move which undoubtedly had a deleterious effect upon the horse's stud career, as breeders were not impressed by his four-year-old record of two failures and a victory over a single opponent in a minor, two-horse race and, having short memories, had by this time forgotten his most important successes of the previous year.

This was evident in the few mares, many of them indifferent, he received in his first two or three seasons. Several of those mares who did go to him were sent as a result of persuasion on my part of their, in some cases rather unwilling, owners. As I always believed that Queen's Hussar would sire winners and that he represented good value, practising what I preached I sent to him Madame Bovary, dam of Belle de Jour, placed second, La Paiva, dam of Brigadier Gerard and Lady Dacre, and Bell Crofts, to whom he bred Eleanor Bold, a two-year-old winner in 1972.

That it would have been worth keeping Queen's Hussar in training until the end of the season is indicated by the four-year-old career of Linacre, whom he had beaten fairly and squarely in the Sussex Stakes in the previous year. Started seven times, Linacre at four won the Scarbrough Stakes at Doncaster, and the Queen Elizabeth II Stakes at Ascot, running second in two good races in France, a race in Ireland and in the Champion Stakes. With a comparable record behind him, Queen's

Hussar would have gone to stud on a much higher plane than he was able to do in the circumstances. It was just as well for me that this was not the case, since I might not have felt like paying the stud fee which he would then have been entitled to command.

It was not until George Blackwell, whose father had the rare distinction of training a winner of the Derby and a winner of the Grand National, Rock Sand and Sergeant Murphy, recently brought up the subject in conversation that I realised that Queen's Hussar might have gone to Australia before La Paiva could have been covered by him. About the end of Queen's Hussar's first season at stud, the Australian jockey George Moore, who was carried to victory in the Derby by Royal Palace, asked George Blackwell if he could find him a stallion for Australia. George suggested that Queen's Hussar would fit the bill and might be for sale, so Moore asked him to find out. George Blackwell got in touch with Peter Nelson, Lord Carnarvon's present trainer, and asked him if he would sound his patron on the matter and let him know the outcome. The reply came back that Queen's Hussar could be bought for £40,000. Meanwhile Lord Carnarvon telephoned George Moore in Australia giving his name as the caller. Moore thinking that someone was pulling his leg, refused to accept the call, and the deal fell through.

6 *Selection in Breeding*

Every breeder has his own ideas about mating mares and, whatever these may be, there is always the factor of luck, which cannot be ignored. All that the breeder can do is to try to arrange matters so that there is a reasonable chance of the right genetic shake-up emerging, and hope for the best. But at least he should know what he is attempting to do; otherwise he might as well put the names of his mares in a hat and pull them out against the list of his nominations. Since some of the most famous horses in Turf history have been bred fortuitously, or even by mistake, there may be something to be said for the system, but in the long run it would almost certainly entail more failures than the method of selection; that is to say, weighing up every aspect, making use only of principles which have scientific backing, endeavouring to correct faults, strengthen weaknesses, preserve a correct balance in temperament and physical attributes, such as speed, stamina, quality, toughness, soundness, confirmation and courage.

It must be appreciated that perfection is virtually unobtainable: the breeder must accept some faults, weigh them against the attributes and, if deciding to go forward with the mating, endeavour to counterbalance them. These were the principles upon which I was endeavouring to work.

From a practical aspect, I am inclined to place pedigree last in designing a mating, because pedigree is only a guide, not a guarantee, since horses with the same pedigree often have completely different genetic compositions, never exactly similar ones. It is only possible to guess at the influences which have emerged in an individual, but unless a breeder has some idea of what influences the important names in a pedigree represent, it is impossible even to guess at their effect.

At the same time, it is dangerous to become a slave to any mating system. To start with, mating racehorses cannot be reduced to hard and fast rules or mathematics, as has been proved by such theories as those evolved by Bruce Lowe and Colonel Vuillier. These are interesting and useful up to a point, but since they are based on unscientific principles they cannot be followed blindly.

By the same token, the work of Dr Franco Varola in dividing the important sires in all parts of the world into categories, according to the nature of the influence which they tend to exert on their offspring, is of value in balancing a pedigree; but it is not, as Dr Varola himself is the first to admit, a prescription for breeding winners.

Regarding the mating of La Paiva with Queen's Hussar on blood lines, the issue was not very complicated, since her pedigree contains remarkably few predominant influences in the early removes.

The advantage of such a pedigree is that if offers great scope in the matter of sires, since there is little danger of arriving at an unbalanced mating, through concentrating too many similar influences in the pedigree, in particular, over-refinement.

It is difficult to convince many breeders that it is possible to 'over-egg the pudding' by concentrating too many influences for high quality in a pedigree. The result tends to be the production of too much nervous energy, producing over-excitability, nervousness or constitutional weakness.

Wealthy businessmen who come into racing and breeding without any knowledge or understanding of it, often seem unable to grasp that 'breeding the best with the best' does not necessarily result in the best; and if offered a mare with an unfashionable pedigree, but good stud prospects, such as Brazen Molly, would as likely as not put the dog on whoever advised them to buy her. This is just as well, since it gives those who study the business the chance of buying a mare worth the money.

The first predominant sire in La Paiva's pedigree is Phalaris, in the third remove. Her sire, Prince Chevalier, is an important and desirable influence, but as a begetter of winners he cannot be compared with Phalaris. The same can be said for the next three sires in this male line, that of St Simon through Persimmon, the sires in question being Prince Rose, Rose Prince and Prince Palatine. This, too, goes for La Paiva's maternal grandsire, Horus, and his male line.

Thus the pedigree of La Paiva was particularly suited, not only to a powerful reintroduction of the influence of Phalaris, but to the introduction of any other similarly important names not present in the first four removes of the pedigree.

The mating with Rockefella, in whose pedigree there is no Phalaris, had disappointed me somewhat, since the outcome, General Wolfe, was well below classic standard. Thus the very powerful concentration in Queen's Hussar of Phalaris, through his best son, Fairway, was most appealing. A further attraction was the introduction of the great line of

Lady Josephine, through Lady Juror, dam of Fair Trial, himself an outstanding sire and a thoroughly desirable influence. But, above all, it was the three lines of Phalaris through Fairway, which intrigued me most in Queen's Hussar's pedigree, so far as blood lines were concerned.

From the pedigree of Brigadier Gerard (see Appendix) it will be seen that there is no inbreeding in the first five removes. The nearest names to appear in the pedigree of both his sire and his dam are Phalaris and Papyrus. Each is to be found in the third remove of La Paiva's pedigree, while Phalaris is present thrice in the fifth remove of Queen's Hussar and Papyrus once, also in the fifth remove.

Another aspect of sending La Paiva to an inexpensive sire such as Queen's Hussar was that, since hitherto she had proved an every other year breeder, it would have been courting fate, financially, to send her to an expensive sire.

It is a fact that many outstanding horses have been foaled when their dams did not have a foal to rear the previous season; that is to say, either they were barren or the foal was born dead. Among the famous winners in this category are Swynford, Sansovino, Colorado, Fairway, Hyperion, Abernant, Solario, Coronach, Saucy Sue, Book Law, Windsor Lad, Dante, Pinza, Ballymoss and Noblesse. For this information I am indebted to an article by Cedric Borgnis in *The British Racehorse* (October Sales Issue, 1970), in which the author examines this occurrence in detail.

However, in this case La Paiva did the opposite, since for the first time she produced a foal in successive years and this one was to prove by far her best. It will be interesting to see the outcome of her mating with Royal Palace (Ballymoss–Crystal Palace, by Solar Slipper) in 1972, for she had no foal that year and Royal Palace is markedly the highest-class stallion with whom she has been mated. Apart from this the mating is, at least from every foreseeable point of view, a sound one.

In 1968, when carrying Brigadier Gerard, La Paiva for the second time went to Major Portion, the outcome being a full brother to Town Major named Brigade Major, who was placed in the last of his three races as a two-year-old, at Newbury, and won twice the following season, including the Cosmopolitan Cup at Lingfield. As a four-year-old he won his only race, the Great Jubilee Handicap at Kempton and then went to New Zealand as a stallion. Like Town Major he is excitable and fidgety, but tough and possessed of considerable ability, though only capable of showing his best form on soft ground. In fact, the mating has worked out with remarkable consistency, indicating the strong trend in La Paiva to throw to the stallion with whom she is mated and reproduce at least some of the influences suggested by the pedigree.

On her way to Newmarket to visit Major Portion at the Egerton Stud, when carrying Brigadier Gerard, La Paiva suddenly became very disturbed, threw herself about the horse box, poured with sweat and got herself into such a state that the box had to be stopped, the mare taken out and put into a farm, where she was treated for cuts and spent the night. She calmed down, was perfectly all right the following day and continued on her journey. I can only think that the foal inside her caused her a spasm of acute discomfort which upset her, for she was an experienced traveller and has never behaved in this way before or since.

La Paiva has come to regard the Egerton Stud as her second home, since apart from visiting Major Portion twice when he was there, she has also twice visited Royal Palace.

7   *The Brigadier enters the Scene*

Early on the morning of 5 March 1968, I had a call from Podmore, the Stud Groom at Egerton, to say that La Paiva had foaled a good bay colt the previous night and that both mare and foal were flourishing. When I saw him I was thrilled. He looked a champion, a beautiful, mahogany bay colt, with black points and a small white star. Strong, perfectly made and full of quality, he had an unusually big eye and a kind, exceptionally intelligent air about him.

He was the best-looking foal at the Egerton Stud that year and, as such, news of him began to get around, helped considerably by propaganda on the part of Queen's Hussar's owner. As Michael Oswald, then Stud Manager at Egerton remarked: 'Everyone got fed up with Lord Carnarvon cracking him up and urging them to go to see him, but those who did so had to admit he was right!'

When any of our mares are in foal, I usually start thinking of suitable names for their offspring, according to their sex, when they will appear. Somehow it never occurred to me that the foal was not going to be a colt and on this presumption I made up my mind to call him Brigadier Gerard. As a boy, Brigadier Gerard had been one of my literary heroes, since I was a keen reader of Conan Doyle's books *The Exploits of Brigadier Gerard* and *The Adventures of Gerard*, whose central character was a gay, dashing and courageous officer in the Hussars de Conflans in Napoleon's army. The name seemed appropriate to the pedigree and when he appeared the colt as time went on seemed, more and more, to take on the character of his namesake. He became handsomer as he grew and developed, while his nature reflected the chivalry, courage, honesty and gentlemanly behaviour which Conan Doyle gave to the hero of these stories.

About midsummer, La Paiva and her foal came home and everyone on the place was filled with admiration at her beautiful colt. They had a paddock to themselves, at first going out at 7.30 in the morning and coming in at dusk then, as the weather became warmer, running out night and day and being fed in the field.

Rightly or wrongly, I believe that the more that thoroughbred stock can run out, provided the paddocks and circumstances are suitable, the more likely they are to become good racehorses. While they are out they wander about, developing their hearts, lungs, limbs and intelligence; accustom themselves to heat, cold, wet, thunder, lightning and flies; find plenty to interest them, whether it is cattle, pheasants on the look-out for leavings from the feed bin, occasionally a fox on the prowl, people working on the stud or vehicles coming and going. In hot weather they prefer to graze at night, as opposed to during the day, but cannot do this if they are in their boxes. Horses that are shut up for the greater part of the day do not have this advantage and, all else equal, are unlikely to do so well on the racecourse.

Much depends upon environment and circumstances and in this respect a small private stud is better placed than a large stud. When there are only half a dozen or so horses to bring in, and they and the men – including the boss – are within easy reach, there is no problem to let them run out until seven or eight o'clock at night; but in a large stud of many horses, with studmen scattered over a wide area, this is not managed so easily, so that it is not uncommon to see mares and young stock being brought in on a blazing hot afternoon at about 3.30 p.m.

To me, half the enjoyment of breeding horses is personal contact with them, making it possible to get to know and understand them individually. This, in turn, gives them confidence and a sense of stability, knowing that they are loved and considered, always having someone behind them. With few horses and good men looking after them, it is possible to spend plenty of time handling them, talking to them and teaching them stable manners.

Each morning, our foals, mares and yearlings are brushed over lightly, have their manes and tails brushed out, their eyes, noses and docks sponged and their feet picked out. At an early stage, the foals are accustomed to wearing a roller and having a bit in their mouth; so that when the time comes for them to go into training they are half broken in. Sometimes we have broken in the yearlings at home, as was the case with Brigadier Gerard.

We like to wean the foals late, at about six months or so, finding that the most satisfactory way is, first, to put the mare and foal each night in adjoining boxes with a grid in between, so that they can see each other, for a week, letting them run together in the paddock during the day; then separate them completely one night, putting in place of the mare the foal who is to be the companion, letting the two foals run together the next day.

There are no hard and fast rules about the treatment of horses, and success can be achieved in many different ways, while horses adapt themselves to the methods of those looking after them. Having found a successful formula, a breeder is inclined to stick to it, and unless it breaks down on him, or he discovers a better one, he is wise maybe to continue in the same way, as it probably suits the circumstances better than any other.

Brigadier Gerard was the only colt foal on the stud, so when the time came to wean him the problem of a companion arose. I did not want to go to the expense of buying a colt foal, which would have to be sold as a yearling and might well show a loss, and I did not know of a colt foal I could borrow – now, I have an arrangement with a friend who has a much larger stud and kindly lets me have a foal as a companion whenever necessary – so I had to think again. Sometimes I have run weaned foals with a quiet hunter – Brigade Major ran with an ex-racehorse, South Grove, who did the job well, the pair becoming fast friends.

When Brigade Major was a yearling, he and South Grove were turned out for a time in a small paddock, on the right as one enters the front gate at East Woodhay House. One morning, between five and six, he started to neigh at the top of his voice and gallop up and down the length of the fence along the drive, as hard as he could go, keeping this up for half an hour or more. Eventually he calmed down and never behaved like this again, nor had he ever done so before. There was no clue, whatever, as to what might have upset him, until 28 December 1972. On this morning, which was my stud groom Hawker's day off, the second man, Myles, was walking back from the yard at 6.10 a.m., having fed the horses. As he approached the gate into the little paddock where Brigade Major had become so distraught, he saw a figure glide through the gate and continue down the drive. When he stopped, it stopped and when he walked on, it glided on, till it reached the front gate and suddenly vanished. The chances are that it was this apparition which had disturbed Brigade Major, though South Grove did not seem affected the same way.

Horses are not often turned out in this paddock and, now, never at night, though in the twenty and more years we have been at East Woodhay House no one had seen the apparition before.

For a companion to Brigadier Gerard I was able to borrow a young pony, about 14.2 hands, from a neighbour, Mr Furniss, who was a retired hunter stud groom and a fine judge of a horse. He produced several horses or ponies for friends of ours and all were a success.

The pony was a very good-looking, strong, intelligent gelding, in colour a rich bay, almost the same hue as the Brigadier and, though representing greatly differing types, they made a well-matched couple and at once became, and remained, very attached to each other. Indeed, I do not think that Brigadier Gerard ever forgot his pony companion; since, some time after he had gone to West Ilsley, Dick Hern remarked to me that the only thing that ever worried the Brigadier was the sight of a pony. This caused him to call out and try to get to it, so much so that if a pony had to pass his box it was necessary to shut the top door in case he caught sight of it. The reason for this may well have been that whenever he saw a pony he associated it with the companion of his yearling days.

It is difficult to determine the extent and nature of a horse's memory. As with humans, it varies according to the individual. I am inclined to believe that recognition depends considerably upon smell and voice; when horses nose each other it is their way of communicating and, in fact, a horse who is difficult to catch can sometimes be approached and secured by sniffing gently at him, when he will sniff back, and then very quietly and gently taking hold of him. There is, of course, the possibility, that he will take exception to your advances and remove a portion of your face; but, so far, this has not happened to me and by this method I have sometimes managed to catch a horse who has proved elusive to all other methods.

Lady Dacre (full sister to Brigadier Gerard) as a foal in 1970

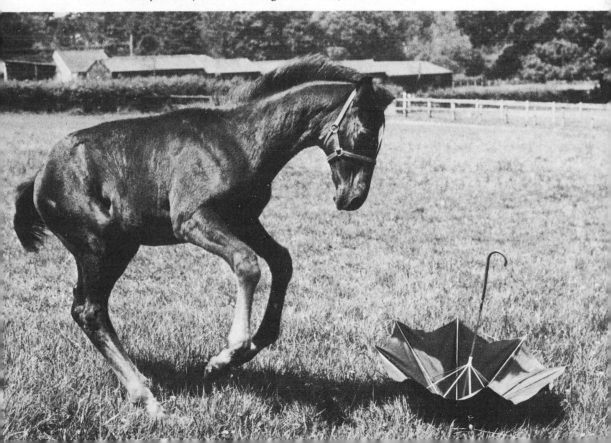

That the memory of a voice can remain for a long time, the Brigadier showed when Myles took his full sister, Lady Dacre, to go into training at West Ilsley, just before the Brigadier left for stud. Myles had not seen the Brigadier since the latter was a yearling, yet as soon as the horse heard his voice he neighed to him. The Brigadier did the same when Dick Hern went to see him during the December Sales, after he had left West Ilsley for good, but this was understandable as he had seen Dick only a few weeks previously.

The Brigadier has always recognised Jean and myself, having seen us frequently since he was a foal; while I led him in and out many times as a foal and yearling, seeing him almost every day until he went into training.

We decided to break the Brigadier at home, partly to save expense in sending him to West Ilsley earlier and partly to have the enjoyment of his company a bit longer. Our stud groom at that time, Cox, who later went back into racing, was a good man with horses, quiet, gentle and an excellent rider – he had been a successful jumping jockey in his younger days. We had handled the Brigadier carefully and thoroughly from the time he was a foal, accustoming him to have bits of tack on him, so that he presented no problem to break. Cox drove him about the stud and when the time came for a saddle to be put on him he humped his back once and thenceforth never put a foot out of place. He would stand like a rock for Cox or me to get on him, and walked and jogged quietly about the stud, allowing me to open and shut the paddock gates, as if he was a seasoned hunter or a trained hack.

In the hope that our impression of the Brigadier would not prove unfounded, I began in my mind to plan his future to a top-level programme. He would have his first race in late May or early June and, if showing the necessary ability, his chief objective would be the Middle Park Stakes at Newmarket. The purpose of this ambitious programme was to find out whether he was good enough to run for the Two Thousand Guineas the following year and, if so, to give him experience of the crucial part of the course, the Dip, which occurs about two furlongs from the finish and which on occasion has determined the result. This was so in the case of Royal Minstrel, whose inability to negotiate the feature as fluently as the winner, Flamingo, cost him the Two Thousand Guineas of 1928. Besides, it would give him experience of spending a night away from home, so that he would be less likely to fret before the Two Thousand than if he had spent the night in a strange stable for the first time.

Consequent to my expressing these high-flown ideas, Jean remarked to me one day: 'If this horse is as good as you think he may be, you know what you'll be offered for him at the end of his two-year-old career?' I said, 'Not really, but it would be a lot of money.'

'A hundred thousand,' she answered. 'But I couldn't afford not to take it,' I countered, to which she replied, 'You'd better make up your mind here and now that you aren't going to take it. You can't do things like that, taking a horse like him away from his trainer; you're not a common coper like ——'

So from that moment, any possibility of the Brigadier being sold vanished for ever. We agreed that, whatever the price, he was not for sale.

In November the Brigadier went off to West Ilsley. From the day he arrived to the day he left, his behaviour was never anything but perfect. As Dick Hern said of him after seeing him do his final gallop for the Middle Park Stakes: 'He always does everything one asks of him, in the nicest possible way.'

He was 'done' by Laurie Williamson, a lad in his early twenties, who had been a milk roundsman but decided he wanted to go into racing and had been taken on by Dick, given a necessarily hurried course in riding and stablemanship and apprenticed. He was a bad rider but a good groom and when allotted Brigadier Gerard cannot have guessed that the decision was to make him the luckiest lad in the yard, a windfall which he repaid by giving Dick a week's notice shortly after he had collected his Christmas money and Brigadier Gerard had retired to stud, despite having been allotted the Brigadier's full sister, Lady Dacre, to do when she arrived as a yearling. However, while the Brigadier was in Williamson's care, he looked after him well.

When the Brigadier left for West Ilsley, he was well grown, but did not strike me as being more than medium sized. I saw little of him during the winter, but on going to visit him when he began serious training in February, I was surprised to see how much he had grown and advanced. Amongst the other two-year-old colts he stood out, not only in looks, but in size, being appreciably bigger than all who were working with him.

The gallops at West Ilsley are excellent, nearly always offering good going at any time of the year; and though standing high up, so that on them it is an overcoat colder than in the valley below and horses trained there tend not to come to hand so early as those working in less exposed surroundings, they enable a trainer to give horses the steady, essential, early work which forms the foundation of a horse's preparation and, in particular, the education of two-year-olds.

By the principles on which I was educated at Clarehaven, it is wise to teach two-year-olds their business and get those who are going to race seriously that season about three parts fit in the spring, when the going is usually good. If horses are left uneducated and unfit while the going is suitable, and then a spell of dry weather comes in, a trainer is left in the position of not being able to progress with his horses at all, or risk breaking them down through working them on firm ground. On the other hand, if horses know the business and are reasonably forward in condition, it is easy to get them racing fit in a short time, as soon as the ground comes right.

Dick Hern works to this pattern, so Brigadier Gerard and the other two-year-old colts at West Ilsley knew their job and were forward enough to do sharp work over three or four furlongs by the second half of March.

On 4 April, Jean and I went over to West Ilsley to see the Brigadier do his first important gallop. This was over four furlongs on the trial ground and comprised seven two-year-old colts; these, apart from Brigadier Gerard, were Rugged (Ribot–Rosalba), Grey Sky (Grey Sovereign–Treacle), Colum (Santa Claus–Mitigation), The Bugler (Klarion–La Bastille), Scar (Relic–Cutle) and Don Magnifico (Star Moss–Floria Tosca).

It was a clear, fresh morning and the Brigadier was ridden by Jimmy Lindley. He started the proceedings by whipping round and dropping Jimmy on the way up to the start. As a two-year-old he had a playful habit of doing this, every now and then, but having achieved his objective, just stood still till he was remounted. He appeared to single out only licensed jockeys to deposit, his other two victims being Joe Mercer and Bobby Elliott, but having put them on the ground once, he seemed content to leave them in peace thereafter.

Waiting at the four-furlong post, Jean, Dick Hern and I knew nothing of this drama, which was just as well. For Jean and I the next few minutes were going to reveal a dream on the way to realisation, or dis-illusion and the possible end of our survival as owner-breeders. From the moment that Brigadier Gerard was born, we had always felt that upon him our whole future in this sphere hung: we would never breed a horse like him again, and if he was not a good one the chances were that hope of our producing such a horse had gone for ever.

The professional in racing learns to control his emotions – 'It might have been worse, I only had £5,000 on him,' that remarkable owner-trainer, Jack Reardon once observed, without a change of expression, in reply to the condolence of a friend upon a defeated gamble – but he must live with his feelings, however tense or bitter these may be.

As I lifted my glasses to focus them on the horses lining up for the start, I could not help the tension of the moment pervading my senses with a blend of excitement and anxiety.

The horses struck off to a level start and before they had gone a furlong it was clear that Jimmy Lindley was going smoothly at the head of the bunch. The nearer they approached the more defined became the Brigadier's advantage, and on reaching us he was a good two lengths clear, with his ears pricked and seeming to be cantering while the others were galloping. Behind, closely bunched, were Grey Sky, Rugged and Colum.

The glow of joy and relief at this impressive performance was tempered by the lessons of past experience: a gallop is only as good as it is proved by form on the racecourse; and until one or more of the horses concerned had run, it was not possible to assess the value of the work in more than terms of conjecture. At the same time, the horses concerned were the most promising of those who, at that time, seemed likely to win as two-year-olds in the stable, so that our immediate reaction was: 'If this isn't a good horse, the others must be very moderate.'

When Jimmy Lindley got back to us after pulling up, he said: 'A very nice colt; he was always going well and will improve a lot; wants a bit of time.' This encouraged us further and we determined to give the Brigadier every chance to develop, by not bringing him out until May or June at the earliest.

The gallop never put him out in any way. He did not fret, never left an oat and pulled out as sound as a bell and fresh as paint the next day.

PART TWO

8 *The Brigadier starts his Racing Career*

Provisionally, I had planned to bring the Brigadier out in the Portsmouth Road Plate at Sandown, on 25 May, the race which his half brother Town Major had won. As it turned out, the Brigadier had a slight temperature a few days before the race and, though it cleared up in twenty-four hours, I would not run him and decided to put him by for a month.

Nothing is more harmful to a horse than to race him when he has any form of illness on him and while, unfortunately, this sometimes cannot be discovered until the damage has been done, any danger sign must be regarded and if an error is to be made it should be on the side of safety.

Meanwhile, there was a spell of dry weather, during which Dick Hern did little with his two-year-old colts other than cantering and steady work over three furlongs, for fear of jarring them. Thus by mid June neither Brigadier Gerard, Rugged, Grey Sky nor Colum had run.

'When are you going to get Brigadier Gerard out? You wanted to run him nearly a month ago and you still haven't done so,' Jean said to me.

While both Dick Hern and I felt that a race would do the Brigadier good, we did not want to risk jarring him by running him on hard ground, but agreed that whenever practicable he should have a race. He was entered in the Berkshire Stakes at Newbury on 24 June, and although a long way from being tuned up was fit enough to run without doing himself any harm, thanks to the foundation of condition laid by his work in the spring. Besides, there is always a good covering of grass at Newbury and, having been well watered, the course was unlikely to jar a horse; officially the going was described as good. So we decided to take the plunge and run him.

Joe Mercer, for many years first jockey at West Ilsley, first to Jack Colling and then, on the latter's retirement, to Dick Hern, rode him.

Joe was in India when the Brigadier had his first gallop, so did not know any more about him than what Jimmy Lindley was able to tell him and from riding him in the steady work he had been doing. Dick Hern gave the Brigadier no chance, as he thought that he could not be forward enough to win, because of the limited amount of work he had done since the spring and the fact that his opponents included three recent winners, one with good form; so much so that he dissuaded his wife, Sheilah, from putting the Brigadier in her jackpot selections.

I had a long-standing engagement to judge at the National Hunter Show at Shrewsbury, so was unable to get to Newbury; but before leaving I remarked to Jean: 'I wouldn't be surprised if this horse doesn't run a lot better than Dick thinks he will, I know the Pretty Polly family so well: they need very little work, and he was three parts fit in the spring and has been doing plenty of steady work since, as well as having to walk up and down hills every day.'

At Shrewsbury I ran into Eddie Griffith, one of the best judges of a horse I know, with whom I had had the privilege of judging at the Stallion Show at Newmarket a year or so before, and by way of conversation said to him: 'I've got a runner today, but I think he's at the wrong meeting; he'd be a certainty in the two-year-old class here, but he runs at Newbury and mightn't be forward enough to win there.'

The Berkshire Stakes, run over five furlongs and worth £1,201 to the winner, drew a field of only five. Favourite at 15 to 8 on was Young and Foolish (Crocket–Wimbledon, by Abernant), a colt belonging to Mr David Robinson, trained by Michael Jarvis and ridden by Lester Piggott. He had won at Newmarket from a big field by two lengths and, in his next and only other start, had run second to Lush Park (Goldhill–Lush Pool, by Dumbarnie), winner of both his two previous races and, subsequently, of the Windsor Castle Stakes at Royal Ascot. The only other runner backed at all seriously was Mais'y Dotes (Tin Whistle–Another Journey, by Royal Charger), who had won four of her six previous races, all in modest company.

Jean went to Newbury in place of me. It had always been agreed tacitly between us that, though we owned the Brigadier in partnership he was 'my' horse and that I should direct the policy governing his career and be the one of us to go into the parade ring: as a professional I do not like making life more difficult for the trainer, officials and others by cluttering up the parade ring with wives, children, friends and such like who, often knowing little of horses, stand a good chance of getting themselves kicked.

Before leaving I asked Jean to tell Joe Mercer to let the horse do his best without giving him a hard race – or getting us warned off by over-doing the latter part of the instruction.

When the time came she said to Joe: 'I was given some instructions to pass on to you, but I've forgotten what they were.' 'That's very helpful,' he said. 'Anyway, you've got a smart dress; almost your racing colours,' Joe added, going on to say, 'Duncan Keith's riding another green one, so I've arranged with him that we'll race together, as the two favourites are sure to be out of the stalls and away before we get going, as they're experienced horses, and if our two horses are left on their own, wide of each other, they'll learn nothing. Unless, of course, I find myself in front!' However, as I had already discussed and agreed the plan with Dick, it made no odds.

Opinions differ greatly as to riding instructions to jockeys. Some owners and trainers issue orders that would fill a volume, others say nothing, some are so incomprehensible in expression that it has been known for a jockey to go out uncertain whether the horse was fancied or not.

From the rider's point of view, I always preferred the trainer or owner to say something, even if it was only 'good bye', a term sometimes applicable to going out on a bad jumper. On this principle, I find the best plan is to agree with the trainer what the jockey is to be told, for one – not both – to give him these instructions, in as brief and lucid terms as possible and always to impress on the jockey that he has complete freedom of action if he has to make a decision in unforeseen circumstances. As often as not, our only orders to Joe Mercer have been 'play it by ear'.

When the Brigadier came into the paddock the first aspect of him that struck Jean was how completely calm he was. He seemed quite impervious to his surroundings, and to have about him that air of majesty which was one of the features which so distinguished him during his racing life. He did not fuss in the parade ring, or when Dick stripped him and put Joe up, but he woke up as he stepped out on to the course and went down to the post fast and impressively. So much so that Henry Porchester, who was naturally interested in the Brigadier since he was by his father's horse Queen's Hussar, rushed down from the stand to back him; by the time he reached the bookmakers the horses had just left the stalls, but he managed to get on.

Though the experienced horses jumped out fastest and led the Brigadier by several lengths, they had not gone a furlong before it was evident to Jean and Dick, who watched the race together, that Joe was very happy in his work: the Brigadier was cantering over his rivals and it

Brigadier Gerard winning his first race, the Berkshire Stakes at Newbury, starting
at 100 to 7, 1970

was only a matter of when Joe let him go. Within the last two furlongs he
gave him the office and the Brigadier at once shot into a lead of eight to
ten lengths. As he approached the winning post, he looked about him in
an interested, inquisitive manner, slowing up a little in the process but still
having a ton in hand and, at the winning post, five lengths to spare.
Second place went to Mais'y Dotes, the horse ridden by Duncan Keith,
Porter's Precinct, being third and the favourite, Young and Foolish,
fourth.

At Shrewsbury I kept wondering how the Brigadier had fared and
could not wait until I got to London and saw the evening paper. When I
read that the Brigadier had won by five lengths I could hardly believe my
eyes: that he should be able to do this in the circumstances showed that,
at the least, he was very useful and might turn out to be top class.

On getting home I heard the story of the race from Jean and Dick, also
Joe Mercer's account. Never given to exaggeration, Joe pronounced himself very pleased with the horse's performance. I observed to Jean that she
seemed to have got on very well without me, which indeed was so.

The day following the Brigadier's victory Colum, who had finished behind him in the gallop, came out for the Kennett Plate at Newbury.

The bookmakers and betting public did not take much notice of the stable's success the previous day, as Colum was allowed to start at 8 to 1, being third favourite. First choice in the betting was Band of Hope (Typhoon–Bandriadore, by Milesian), who had run second the previous Newbury meeting to Swing Easy (Delta Judge–Free Flowing), an American-bred colt belonging to Jock Whitney and trained by Jeremy Tree, who had gone on to win the New Stakes at Royal Ascot. The form read well, so it is not surprising that Band of Hope, trained at Arundel by John Dunlop, was hot favourite at 13 to 8. He ran well, but not well enough, as Joe Mercer brought Colum to the front approaching the last furlong and won comfortably by three lengths. This raised our hopes still higher, as we knew that the Brigadier was better than Colum.

The next matter was to decide upon the Brigadier's future programme. He thrived after the race, which clearly had brought him on, and he held several engagements likely to suit him. The choice lay between the July Stakes at Newmarket on 8 July or the Champagne Stakes at Salisbury on 2 July.

The July Stakes presented the attraction of being six days further away than the Champagne Stakes, but it had a more formidable entry, including Swing Easy, and entailed a fairly long journey with a night away from home. At Salisbury, on the other hand, the opposition was weak and the course only a short distance from West Ilsley.

I was anxious to give the Brigadier as easy a race as possible, at the same time widening his experience in order to fit him for the time when he would have to meet good horses; so decided upon the Champagne Stakes at Salisbury which, like the July Stakes, is run over six furlongs.

The Brigadier carried a penalty for his success in the Berkshire Stakes, which brought his weight up to 9 st 7 lb. He was favourite at 13 to 8 on, next in the betting being Gaston Again (Weeper's Boy–Ballymiss, by Luminary), a filly trained by George Beeby and winner of her previous race, a maiden plate at Lingfield, by four lengths.

There appeared to be no fancy for any of the other runners. The race was started from a barrier, as opposed to stalls as at Newbury, but Dick's horses are always well schooled to both and I had no fears of the Brigadier being disconcerted by a different form of start. As I was seeing him on the racecourse for the first time, it was a particularly exciting and interesting event for me.

When the Brigadier came into the paddock I felt proud of him: he looked a different class to his opponents, even though these included the good–looking Comedy Star (Tom Fool–Latin Walk), a very handsome colt bred in the U.S.A. and later a high–class miler.

'What do you think of him?' I remarked to Ron Smyth, the Epsom trainer and former champion N. H. rider, who was standing beside me at the parade ring rail. 'A good sort. Is he a shade light of bone?', he said. This was an interesting observation, since the quality of the Brigadier's limbs gives them a deceptively slender look, when in fact he has eight and a half inches of bone below the knee.

His behaviour was impeccable, he went down to the post with a sweeping, majestic stride and gave no trouble at the start. When the gate went up, Joe settled the Brigadier in behind the leaders and was content to remain there until about a furlong and a half from home, at which stage he moved easily into a clear lead. On finding himself in front he took stock of his surroundings and, perhaps feeling lonely in splendid isolation, veered across to the rails. He did this on more than one occasion, seeming to like running along the rails, but was well clear of Gaston Again, his nearest rival, so there was no danger of an objection. Joe kept him going

Brigadier Gerard winning the Champagne Stakes at Salisbury, 1970

with his hands and the Brigadier's powerful, rhythmic stride took him to an easy victory by four lengths.

The impression he gave me was that he was still immature, with a great deal of scope for improvement, and that he might not reach his best until he was four. The sharp six-furlong course at Salisbury, some of it downhill and the early part on the bend, did not suit his long stride and slight knee action, underlining the impression of immaturity and lack of racing experience. Time was to show that the Brigadier was at his best at Ascot, on the round course, where the uphill run-in fitted his action to perfection.

A day or so after the Champagne Stakes I was chatting to Buster Haslam, Dick Hern's travelling head lad, about the Brigadier, his race at Salisbury and how he had done after it. He told me the horse had travelled well and eaten up, but had weaved in his box when he got home, which Dick Hern confirmed to me later. This was a matter for consideration. Though calm and tough, both mentally and physically, the Brigadier has always been sensitive, intelligent and observant, able to work things out for himself; so that the fact that he had weaved – paced from side to side with his forelegs, while standing still on his hind legs   was significant. It meant that he was thinking over his race, perhaps saying to himself: 'I wonder if I'm going to do this every week.' Whatever the thoughts passing through his head, it seemed wise to let him settle down completely in his mind before he had another race; on the principle that a child who has become over-excited after going to a party should be allowed to calm down and forget about it before going to another one.

Consequently he did not race again for over six weeks, doing only routine work in the meanwhile. Thus he had plenty of time to forget about the excitement of his two races in quick succession; and having stopped weaving in a day, he had no occasion to start doing so again. He has always been prone to weave slightly, for instance, after having been got ready to go out at exercise he is standing tied up in his box waiting for the call to pull out, but the habit has never taken hold of him: it is more an expression of impatience than of anxiety.

Though in many ways so calm and gentle, the Brigadier is highly sensitive, with an awareness which makes him suspicious of anything strange or hinting of danger.

One day, soon after he arrived at West Ilsley, there was a bad thunderstorm over the stables; it continued in force for a considerable period, with thunder, lightning and heavy rain. He was loose in the box at the time, and when his lad came to catch him he was quite unable to do so; the

Brigadier quietly, but determinedly turned his quarters to him at every attempt. Finally with patience and help, he was secured. The same thing happened after another thunderstorm, when he proved even more difficult to catch; so much so that for several weeks he was permanently attached to a line across his box which enabled him to lie down and get up as he pleased, but kept him tethered. He took no exception to this arrangement, becoming quite accustomed to it. When he began to do regular cantering work, this trait disappeared and he was taken off the line and returned to ordinary routine; but for a while he remained suspicious of being caught and once, when I went to see him and his lad was not in the yard, he did not want Geordie Campbell, the head lad, to take hold of him, but allowed me to do so, probably because he had known me all his life.

It seems likely that the trouble started because he was afraid of being tied up during the thunderstorms, in case of fire or some other disaster occurring when he was secured and unable to escape.

For some reason, when he was being boxed up to go to Salisbury, the Brigadier decided that he did not want to go in forwards, but showed no objection to going in backwards. Thenceforth he elected to go in backwards, until he came to be boxed up after the Eclipse Stakes, when he went in forwards of his own accord. In his last two or three races he opted for going in forwards, as he did when leaving West Ilsley for the Egerton Stud.

After the Brigadier went into training some warts appeared round the side of his mouth. These were in a bad place because the bit rubbed against some of them, causing them to bleed. They were charmed away by a friend, Syd Mercer, a successful owner and trainer after the war, who brought off some lucrative gambles and retired about half a dozen years ago. A good man to hounds and as a point-to-point rider in his day, whom I had known since pre-war days at Clarehaven, Syd discovered his ability to charm away warts, by mistake.

He bought a hunter at Tattersalls' Knightsbridge Sale, which used to take place every Monday, getting him cheap because he was covered in warts; but he was a good sort, and as Syd had not much money to spend he took a chance with this affliction. When he got the horse home he went into his box and stood looking at the warts and thinking about them, for they were a formidable array. After a day or two, when he was looking at the horse at stable time, he noticed with astonishment that the warts seemed to be disappearing and, gradually, they went away altogether.

Syd treated Brigadier Gerard in the same way and, before long, the warts vanished.

Apart from the gallop in March, Brigadier Gerard was never tried. We did not want to bet on him, because if he turned out top class there was no need to do so; and horses can be ruined or soured by asking them too much at home. Wisely, Dick believes in keeping his horses fresh and happy once they are fit, which on training grounds such as West Ilsley, which are undulating and thus make a horse use his muscles even when walking, does not entail giving them as much work as on flat ground such as Newmarket.

The Brigadier was always clean winded, as his first race showed, and during the whole of his racing career he did only normal, orthodox work. If his training had any salient characteristic it was that he was never worked long distances, always at least a furlong shorter than the distance of the race which was his immediate objective. Even when he had to run for the first and only time over a mile and a half, in the King George VI and the Queen Elizabeth Stakes at Ascot, when he was four, he did not go more than seven to eight furlongs in his preparation for it. In keeping to this principle, Dick Hern was in my view absolutely right, because nothing blunts a horse's speed more than fast work over long distances. In fact, Dick's whole handling of the Brigadier's training was a copy-book example of how a racehorse should be prepared for his engagements.

Though at Salisbury the Brigadier had given me the impression that he would stay a mile well, and I had entered him in several seven-furlong races such as the Solario Stakes and the Horris Hill Stakes, in case he lacked top-class speed, I made up my mind to keep him to six furlongs as a two-year-old.

I remember Fred Darling telling me that he was against running his prospective Two Thousand Guineas and Derby horses beyond six furlongs when they were two-year-olds, so as not to take the edge off their speed or get on top of them, which can be done in heavy going or by a hard race.

With a prospective Guineas horse, especially, this is a wise plan. Horses such as Nijinsky, who won the Dewhurst Stakes (seven furlongs) and Sir Ivor, successful in the Grand Criterium (one mile), have won the Two Thousand, but each had a great deal in hand and won these races without being pressed. A hard race over six furlongs is not so gruelling an ordeal for a two-year-old as one over a mile, especially for a horse who is bred to be a miler.

For one who has a true staying pedigree it is a different matter. In fact, such a horse may well find it less of a strain to race over seven furlongs or a mile than over six furlongs, particularly, if he is not a quick beginner.

On this basis, the Middle Park Stakes is the ideal two-year-old target for a Two Thousand Guineas horse, the Dewhurst Stakes or the Observer Gold Cup for a Derby-cum-St Leger horse.

The system upon which I make entries is to give the trainer a free hand to enter them where he likes, sending him a list of the races in which I want them entered. In this way a suitable entry is unlikely to be missed. A sensible, competent trainer can be relied upon not to throw money away on unduly prolific or absurd entries, and will sometimes notice a race which the owner has failed to do, and vice versa. Dick Hern and I have found that this system works well.

As regards planning, an owner should never go against his trainer in the matter of his horse's soundness or well being. If the career of the horse is the first consideration, the plan must be suited to the horse, not the horse to the plan.

In the case of horses below the top class, there must be some give and take between owners in a public stable. There is no object in two owners hitting their heads together for £250 at a Wolverhampton evening meeting, when by going different ways each might win with their respective horses; but with top horses and top races, so far as I am concerned, it is each man for himself, whether it means clashing with another owner in the stable or not. It is only once in a lifetime that the average owner is likely to be fortunate enough to possess a top notcher and when this stroke of luck comes his way he is entitled to make the most of it.

It is comparatively seldom that such clashes occur, and in the whole of the Brigadier's career none of his engagements crossed the interests of another owner in the stable.

The race we chose for the Brigadier's next appearance was the Washington Singer Stakes, six furlongs, at Newbury on 15 August, worth £1,154. It appeared to suit our purpose well. He knew the course, which was barely half an hour's journey from his stable, the opposition was unlikely to be formidable and he had had plenty of time to settle down and continue to develop physically after his previous race, and the going was good.

In the meantime, Grey Sky, who had been beaten by the Brigadier in the gallop, had won at Goodwood and Salisbury, while the day before the Brigadier was due to run Rugged, who had finished second in the gallop, won at Newbury. The form was working out well. It was hardly surprising, therefore, that the Brigadier was an odds on favourite at 4 to 9.

There were only five runners, next in the betting being Hello (I Say–Ista Jill, by Gratitude), who had won two of his only three races, followed by

Takasaki, Comedy Star and High Command, all maidens, receiving only 6 lb from the Brigadier, by reason of the modest value of his two previous victories.

It was clear that the Brigadier had progressed since his last race. He had muscled up and strengthened, and looked a fit racehorse who knew what he was about, as opposed to the immature, inexperienced juvenile of his first two races.

The Brigadier was drawn number three of the five runners and did not leave the gate quite as fast as Hello and Comedy Star. Joe was content to settle him in behind, as he had done in his first race and at Salisbury. One could see he was moving easily and well. At the distance, Joe started looking for an opening, but the horses in front of him were closely bunched and I began to wonder whether he would get through. Eventually an opening appeared and in an instant Joe had gone for it; in a couple of strides he was through. By this time there was barely a furlong to go, but the race was over: the Brigadier moved smoothly and effortlessly into a two-length lead and that was that. Comedy Star, Takasaki and Hello followed him home.

It was a fluent, professional, rather than a spectacular performance and not all the critics were impressed; but we were more than satisfied, for he had not had the clearest of runs, yet had shown a spark of true brilliance, enabling him to make the fullest use of the slender tactical opportunity which presented itself; moreover, he had plenty in reserve at the finish.

When he got off, Joe remarked: 'I don't know what this horse is; all I know is that when I ask him he just goes "ping" and he's there.'

The Brigadier thrived after the race and did not fret, so the policy of giving him time to settle down after his race in the Champagne Stakes clearly had paid off. This policy was followed throughout his first two seasons, with the result that he developed so much confidence that, by the time he was four, we could have raced him once a week without his turning a hair.

It is impossible to make hard and fast rules about horses. The Bard, who had the misfortune to be foaled the same year as Ormonde, was unbeaten in all his sixteen races as a two-year-old, starting with the Brocklesby Stakes at Lincoln in March, ran second to Ormonde in the Derby, won the Doncaster Cup and several other races as a three-year-old, his only defeat apart from the Derby being when he failed to give 31 lb to Riversdale in the Manchester Cup.

But The Bard was a small, neat, compact horse who came to hand early, whereas the Brigadier was big, immature and did not reach his full strength and development until he was four. Even allowing that The Bard was not extended in any of his races during his first season, had the Brigadier been faced with a similar programme he would not have trained on as he did. It is also significant that The Bard did not race as a four-year-old.

9 *The First Big Test*

With three easy victories behind him, the Brigadier had now acquired the experience, confidence and physical development to fit him for his final, crucial test of the season, the Middle Park Stakes at Newmarket. This would tell us whether he was up to classic standard, or not, and enable us to plan his three-year-old career accordingly.

At heart I have always been a Newmarket man, having spent the first five years of my racing life there. Its whole atmosphere is imbued with Turf history, its racecourse offers the finest test of a flat racer and jockey in the world, and the wide sweeping stretch of the Heath rolling away into the distance on either side of the town, has a nobility and awe about it which never ceases to thrill me.

Likewise, to win its traditional races, with the great names inscribed on their roll of winners, has always been among my most cherished ambitions, particularly the Guineas and the Middle Park Stakes. In some ways I would rather win the Two Thousand than the Derby, and of all the two-year-old races in the Calendar there is none I would rather win than the Middle Park. Though we never won the Middle Park at Clarehaven in my time, the stable had done so thrice in earlier days, with Galvani, Flair, who won the One Thousand the following year, and the great Pretty Polly herself. Besides, it offered the perfect introduction to the Guineas, as shown by the excellent record in the Two Thousand of horses who have won or been placed in the Middle Park. Since the war, Nearula, Our Babu, Right Tack and Brigadier Gerard have all won both races, while Khaled, Saravan, The Cobbler, Abernant, King's Bench, Major Portion and Petingo are Middle Park winners who finished second in the Two Thousand.

The form continued to work out well, for Comedy Star won next time out, at Chester, as did Hill Command at Yarmouth.

With the Middle Park some ten weeks ahead, the Brigadier again had plenty of time to relax after his race and he went from strength to strength.

Joe Mercer nearly always rode him in his fast work, otherwise his usual partner at exercise was Bob Turner, a first-class rider, strong, quiet, cool and secure, which is more than can be said for a good many lads these days, due to the pointless fashion of riding exaggeratedly short.

By this time another good two-year-old had revealed himself in the stable. This was Brook Holliday's imposing bay colt, Fine Blade (Fortino II–Cursorial, by Crepello).

On 19 September, Brigadier Gerard, Fine Blade and Mild Winter worked six furlongs, Joe Mercer riding Fine Blade and Bobby Elliott Brigadier Gerard. They came a real good gallop on the bit, with the Brigadier going appreciably the better at the finish.

On 25 September, Fine Blade made his first appearance, in the Waterford Stakes at Ascot, which he won narrowly but convincingly from Velvet Cap (Major Portion–Covert Side, by Abernant), winner of his previous race, a maiden race at Goodwood, from Royalty (Relko–Fair Bid, by My Babu) a colt trained by Dick Hern for Lady Beaverbrook and a pretty good one the following season. This was encouraging for the Brigadier's prospects in the Middle Park.

After the Middle Park, Fine Blade won the Duke of Edinburgh Stakes at Ascot by a comfortable two and half lengths and then ran a creditable third to Linden Tree (Crepello–Verbena, by Vimy) and Minsky, a full brother to Nijinsky, in the Observer Gold Cup.

I had not ridden the Brigadier since he was a yearling and was interested to see how he had developed in the meantime and what sort of feel he gave me, so asked Dick if I could ride him a half speed one day. He agreed and I did so about a fortnight before the Middle Park. Not surprisingly, the difference in him was very great. He had filled out, grown, lengthened and developed all round; it felt more as if I was on a three-year-old than a two-year-old. I went five furlongs behind a two-year-old belonging to Jakie Astor, The Bugler, who is now a successful hurdler, trained by his owner. I must have been giving The Bugler about two stone.

The Brigadier, even at this stage of his career, was an imposing horse to sit on. In contrast to Ormonde, whose owner the Duke of Westminster found him an uncomfortable 'downhill' ride, the Brigadier was superb. He has a great front, strong, with beautifully moulded shoulders, a smooth effortless stride and a good mouth, taking a nice hold without pulling or hanging. Altogether he gave an impression of unusual power, balance and rhythm, together with the ability to quicken instantly. Being accustomed to start off at a steady pace and increase speed over the last two furlongs, he took a stronger hold as he approached this point and I dearly would have liked to have eased him out and let him really go; but with some ten stone on his back this, while enjoyable for me, would not have been to his benefit, so I kept him behind The Bugler till we pulled up.

Opinions formed from riding a horse in an exercise gallop can be deceptive, but the feel given me by the Brigadier was that he was top class; it remained to be seen whether this would be confirmed on the racecourse.

Shortly before the Middle Park Stakes, Dick considered moving the Brigadier up to the security box in the front yard, which eventually he occupied for the remainder of his time at West Ilsley; but he decided against it, on the grounds that it would be unwise to risk upsetting him before the race by such a change. It was a fortunate decision since, when he was moved to his new box after the Middle Park Stakes, he got cast and bumped his knees. Though the injury was minor and temporary, had it occurred just before the Middle Park he would not have been able to run in it.

In his final work for the Middle Park Stakes, the Brigadier went better than ever; he seemed to improve as the year progressed, not only in his work but also in looks. On 26 September he gave an easy beating to Grey Sky and a good filly of Brook Holliday's, Madame's Share; and in his final work over four furlongs, three days later, he left his companion, Hunting Tower, standing after going fifty yards.

The Brigadier travelled well to Newmarket, settled down in the racecourse stables and ate up every oat. In the morning, he pulled out fresh and in the peak of condition, ready to run for his life. It was a beautiful, sunny, crisp, autumn day, the course in perfect condition, forming an appropriate setting for what is sometimes called the two-year-old Derby.

There were five runners, those facing the Brigadier being Swing Easy, who in his last race had finished third to the unbeaten My Swallow (Le Levanstell–Darrigle, by Vilmoray) in the seven-furlong Prix de la Salamandre at Longchamp; Mummy's Pet (Sing Sing–Money for Nothing, by Grey Sovereign), a very fast colt bred by that competent and stylish amateur rider, Tim Holland-Martin, from the brilliant sprinting family of Farthing Damages, dam of Whistler, and winner of all his three races, notably the Hyperion Stakes and the Norfolk Stakes; Fireside Chat, a fast American-bred colt with good form, and Renoir Picture, a maiden of little distinction.

Though Swing Easy's only defeat had been over seven furlongs, a distance probably too far for him, at the hands of My Swallow, the out-

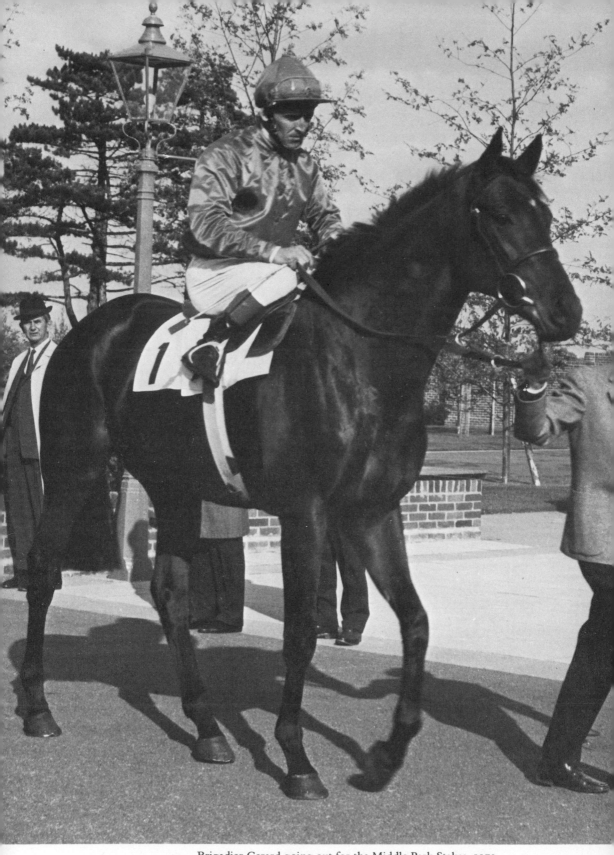

Brigadier Gerard going out for the Middle Park Stakes, 1970

standing two-year-old of the season and conqueror, narrowly and perhaps luckily, of Mill Reef in the Prix Robert Papin, Mummy's Pet from John Sutcliffe junior's Epsom stable was favourite at 6 to 5 on, with Swing Easy at 9 to 4 and Brigadier Gerard, who had opened at 11 to 2, starting at 9 to 2. Geoff Lewis was on Mummy's Pet, Lester Piggott rode Swing Easy.

When he strode into the paddock, Brigadier Gerard 'above the rest in shape and gesture proudly eminent stood like a tower', to borrow a line from *Paradise Lost*, appropriate even though it refers to Satan. He looked a king and caught more than one astute eye, including that of Nico Collin, who said to me: 'That's a proper horse of yours, he stands out on looks and I've gone and backed him on the strength of it.'

Fireside Chat was the first to hit the front, setting only a fair pace. Swing Easy and Brigadier Gerard came next with Geoff Lewis holding up Mummy's Pet to conserve the brilliant speed he had displayed in his previous races.

Joe Mercer knew that Brigadier Gerard stayed every yard of the trip; and when after two furlongs he realised that Fireside Chat was setting a pace which could only play straight into the hands of Mummy's Pet, he sent the Brigadier along. In two or three strides he had shot into a clear lead and that was the last his opponents saw of him. When he reached the winning post he was three lengths to the good with his ears pricked. Mummy's Pet just got the better of Swing Easy by half a length for second place, Fireside Chat and Renoir Picture following them in, some way behind.

Brigadier Gerard winning the Middle Park Stakes, 1970, from Mummy's Pet and Swing Easy

It was a truly thrilling moment. To have won the Middle Park Stakes was a triumph in itself, but for the Brigadier to have slaughtered the opposition in this way was unbelievable. His right to contest the Two Thousand Guineas had been won with honours.

The Brigadier's victory was received by the critics, generally, either in the light of considerable surprise or in that of the belief that it was not top-class form. To a man, they thought that the Middle Park field was not in the same class as the two colts who had filled the limelight of the two-year-old stage, Mr David Robinson's My Swallow, an imposing, powerful, bay colt by Le Levanstell, and Mr Paul Mellon's beautiful, neat, American-bred colt, also a bay, Mill Reef (Never Bend–Milan Mill, by Princequillo). My Swallow, who was bred in Ireland by Mr Myles Walshe, had won all his seven starts, among them the French two-year-old classics, the Prix Robert Papin, the Prix Morny and the Grand Criterium, as well as the Prix de la Salamandre and the Prix du Bois, a feat never accomplished before. His remaining victories were the Zetland Stakes at York and the Woodcote Stakes at Epsom.

Mill Reef finished the season with six wins from seven starts, including the Coventry Stakes at Royal Ascot, the Gimcrack Stakes at York and the Imperial Stakes at Kempton. His one defeat was in the Prix Robert Papin, in which he failed by a short head against My Swallow, from an unfavourable draw, having travelled badly and eaten sparingly. These considerations suggested that, at his best, Mill Reef was the better of the two.

Few people could believe that owner-breeders operating on so modest a scale as ourselves could have produced a true champion. The late William Hill, a keen observer of any horse likely to develop into a classic winner, with a view to his firm's ante-post book, leaned over the rails and said to me as I stood in the winner's enclosure: 'What do you think? Not top-class form is it?' Hardly able to credit being the part owner-breeder of a colt who had won in the style of a future Two Thousand winner, and in view of Mill Reef and My Swallow not having opposed the Brigadier, I replied: 'You're probably right. It looks as if it was a sub-standard Middle Park.' But not everyone thought this way. George Cracknell, formerly our travelling lad at Clarehaven and now retired, came up to me full of enthusiasm: 'John, you'll win the Guineas for sure. This horse is a smasher. Look at the scope he's got for improvement and the way he murdered that lot and came back as fresh as paint.' As the Brigadier stood in the unsaddling enclosure, proud, calm and triumphant I felt that George was right. At that moment there was not a prouder or happier man in the world.

When I returned home and came down to earth I began to go through the form book with a tooth-comb, to try to evaluate the Brigadier's performance in relation to Mill Reef and My Swallow, whom I rated within a pound of each other, Mill Reef the better of the two.

Fourth in the Middle Park Stakes, five and a half lengths behind Brigadier Gerard, was Fireside Chat. In his first race, Fireside Chat had spreadeagled a huge field at Newmarket, despite losing much ground at the start. Next time out he appeared in the Salisbury Stakes, which was the occasion of Mill Reef's debut. Fireside Chat was giving Mill Reef 7 lb and was beaten decisively by four lengths. On the basis of calculating 3 lb being equal to a length, Mill Reef came out 5 lb in front of Fireside Chat, whereas Brigadier Gerard came out a fraction over 16 lb in front of Fireside Chat.

Between these two races Fireside Chat ran twice, finished third to Blue Butterfly and Dulcet, giving the former 5 lb and meeting the latter at level weights, allowing for weight for sex, and second in the Norfolk Stakes at Doncaster to Mummy's Pet at level weights, beaten one and a half lengths, a length closer to Mummy's Pet than in the Middle Park Stakes.

Even allowing for Mill Reef improving after his first race and Fireside Chat deteriorating, it was arguable that Brigadier Gerard was in front of Mill Reef.

The link between the Brigadier and My Swallow came through Swing Easy. In the Middle Park, the Brigadier beat Swing Easy by three and a half lengths. In the Prix de la Salamandre, seven furlongs, My Swallow beat Swing Easy by exactly the same distance; but it was palpably evident, and subsequently confirmed, that Swing Easy did not stay this distance, so that over six furlongs he would undoubtedly have finished a good deal closer to My Swallow; on this premise, Brigadier Gerard was better than My Swallow.

Added to this, the Brigadier had several advantages over both Mill Reef and My Swallow: he did not come out until 24 June, whereas My Swallow had his first race on 12 May, Mill Reef his on 13 May. He had only four races, as against Mill Reef's seven and My Swallow's seven. He never had a hard race – My Swallow and Mill Reef had a real bender in the Robert Papin. He had very little travelling, which often takes more out of a horse than racing – My Swallow went five times to France, Mill Reef once and both journeyed to York. Besides, the Brigadier was more immature than both Mill Reef and My Swallow, therefore being entitled to make relatively greater improvement from two to three years.

This gave us every reason to hope that, at least, the Brigadier had a good chance of beating both Mill Reef and My Swallow, if all three arrived at the post for the Two Thousand fit and well.

When an owner of modest means finds himself in possession of a good horse, it is taken for granted that such a horse can be bought at a price, on the principle that if the owner holds on to it he must either be a lunatic or a martyr to *folie de grandeur*. So that, soon after the Brigadier had showed himself to be a horse of ability and promise, we began to be approached as to the possibility of our selling him. One of the first to do this was Jeremy Tree on behalf of Jock Whitney, who had been at Newbury when the Brigadier won the Berkshire Stakes – the same meeting at which Swing Easy won for Jock – and had been impressed both by our colt's looks and potential. As an owner-breeder of experience and a rider himself, Jock knows a horse when he sees one and deserves credit for his astute appreciation of the Brigadier at this early stage of his career. However, so far as we were concerned, the die was already cast: the horse was not for sale.

Our final temptation came when one of the bloodstock agencies telephoned to ask whether we would consider selling the horse, adding that their client was prepared to pay a very high price. I took the call and explained that the Brigadier could not be bought at any price.

A couple of days later I received a letter, which I have kept as a matter of historic interest, saying that the agency had been authorised to offer us £250,000 for Brigadier Gerard. When I read it, I felt quite ill: it was a figure far outside our financial aura, representing indefinite security for ourselves and our two boys in affluence and comfort for the rest of our lives. But, perhaps luckily, because few can guarantee resistance to the attraction of such financially glittering lures, the irrevocable decision at which we had arrived already placed us beyond temptation; so the offer was turned down.

It did not stop prospective buyers trying to persuade us to part with the Brigadier. As time went on, offers of blank cheques came in, if not like confetti, with tedious regularity, up to his four-year-old season. So much so that we were constrained to publish an announcement to the effect that the Brigadier could not be bought. Only then did they cease for good.

When the Two-Year-Old Free Handicap was published, it read as follows: My Swallow 9 st 7 lb, Mill Reef 9 st 6 lb, Brigadier Gerard 9 st 5 lb. This was an assessment with which few could disagree. Though, as expounded earlier, it could be argued that Brigadier Gerard came out as good as My Swallow and better than Mill Reef on the mathematical interpretation of form, the record of the latter pair was more imposing than that of the Brigadier. At the same time, had the late Jockey Club Handicapper, Geoffrey Freer, the high-priest of handicapping, been alive, it would not have surprised me had he placed the Brigadier top. For he was a man not be be deluded by prestige alone; he related factual perform-ance to an uncanny insight to a horse's potential and he was seldom wrong.

10 *Prelude to the Two Thousand*

During that winter the Brigadier grew and thrived. As a two-year-old he had measured 16.1 hands, but by the time he had begun his three-year-old racing season he was 16.2, at which height he has remained.

Though a very good doer, he did not become at all gross during the winter; the weight he put on was strictly in proportion to his growth. Like his sire, Queen's Hussar, and Fairway, of whom he has three lines in his pedigree, the Brigadier shows no sign of becoming coarse or unduly heavy as a stallion.

In the off season, Dick Hern's horses have a spell away from the gallops, trotting on a road which Jakie Astor had built on part of the estate or, in bad weather, in the covered ride. About the last week in January or the beginning of February they start cantering work. Unless a horse is to be

Stud yard at East Woodhay House

West Ilsley racing stables

aimed, specifically, at the Lincolnshire Handicap or another early engagement, this is quite early enough.

By this time the Brigadier had built up into a truly magnificent individual, the perfect model of a three-year-old racehorse. His temperament had remained unaltered; indeed, as he grew older he became even more composed and settled. After his two-year-old season, I never recall hearing of him dropping his shoulder or whipping round on the gallops, as occasionally he had done the previous year; he seemed to realise that as he gained seniority in the yard it was due to him to behave in an exemplary and responsible manner.

From the time the Brigadier won the Middle Park Stakes, I began to give thought to his programme as a three-year-old. The first question was whether or not to give him a race before the Two Thousand Guineas. The choice of races lay between the Greenham Stakes at Newbury, the Usher Stakes at Kempton, the Ascot Two Thousand Guineas Trial, the Craven Stakes at Newmarket and the Thirsk Classic Trial.

Since Mill Reef was to run in the Greenham and My Swallow at Kempton, there was nothing to be gained by taking either of them on, thereby subjecting the Brigadier to what was likely to be a Two Thousand Guineas battle before the big day.

The Ascot race was too early in the year. The earlier a horse is raced in the season, the less likely is he to maintain his form to the end; and since I was particularly anxious to run the Brigadier in the Champion Stakes in October, to find out whether he stayed a mile and a quarter, with a view to planning his four-year-old season, I had no wish to dissipate his autumnal form by running him in a minor race so soon. The Craven Stakes entailed giving weight away and was also rather early; and Thirsk meant too long a journey. Apart from all this, the Brigadier had shown that he could win without a preliminary race; this aspect had been underlined by his victory first time out, without a preparation.

Therefore I decided to send the Brigadier to run for the Two Thousand without racing him beforehand. I had complete confidence in Dick Hern's ability to get him fit, and when I put the plan to him and to Joe Mercer they agreed to it.

One of the great qualities of Dick Hern as a trainer is that he never loses his sense of proportion over horses; they are treated according to their individual requirements, regardless of status. Some trainers think that because they have a classic horse he must be given twice as much work as an ordinary horse, whether he requires it or not; with the result that by the time they have finished with him he is no longer a classic horse. The Brigadier was always a completely normal horse in his requirements as regards being prepared for a race; consequently, his training was strictly orthodox. When he became famous, the Press were always asking Dick what special treatment he received in the way of training and feeding, and it was difficult to convince them that he had none.

By the same token, just because he had a Two Thousand candidate who was due to go into the race without a previous run, Dick was not deluded into starting to work him before he would do so in the ordinary course of events.

Thus I was not displeased to read in the training reports, which admittedly are not always accurate, that My Swallow was doing fast work as early as February, since this betokened the possibility of the edge being

East Woodhay House, Newbury

off him by the time he got to the post for the Two Thousand itself.

In a large stable of horses, it is not difficult to arrange the work for the mutual benefit of a classic three-year-old and some of the older horses. The reason for this is that, however good he is, the three-year-old is 16 lb behind a four-year-old over six furlongs in April at weight-for-age, so that a reasonably good four-year-old can be put to work with a classic three-year-old at weights adjusted to be detrimental to neither. In any case, they should never be required to work off the bit, in which case even if the weights are unfavourable to one or the other no harm will be done.

In the Brigadier's three-year-old season the stable were well equipped with useful older horses, in particular Duration (Only for Life–Tikki Tavi, by Honeyway), Miracle (High Hat–Miss Klaire II, by Klairon) and Richboy (Princely Gift–Riches, by Rockefella). These three were his chief working companions, sometimes together, sometimes separately and on occasions accompanied by one of the three-year-olds, such as Rugged, Colum or Grey Sky.

That the three older horses came to no great harm as a result is shown by Duration winning six races, Miracle two and Richboy one – he also carried 9 st into fourth place in the Cambridgeshire, only a short head and a head behind the second. Each was successful in at least one good-class race and was also several times placed.

The Brigadier's usual days for fast work were Tuesday and Saturday, when as a rule he was ridden by Joe Mercer. They became very fond of each other, forming a close understanding, comparable to the great partnership between Steve Donoghue and Brown Jack, which in the Queen Alexandra Stakes at Ascot saw victory no less than six times running. Joe used to talk to him a lot, as if he were human, and I am sure that this helped to imbue the Brigadier with a confidence in Joe, which enabled him to do his very best for him on the racecourse and, in times of stress, as in the St James's Palace Stakes and the Champion Stakes of 1971, tip the scales between defeat and victory.

Horses are very susceptible to voice: they may not understand what is being said to them, in the strict sense of the word, but the meaning gets through to them. Some years ago the late John de Moraville once told me that a chaser came over from France to him and he could not get the horse to thrive. He stood miserably in his box, left most of his food and took no interest in his work. One day John hit on the idea of putting a French lad to do him, and as soon as he heard French spoken to him the horse took on a new lease of life, started to eat heartily, work well and to win races.

One of the salient points about the Brigadier's work at home was its consistency; he always worked in the same way, doing exactly what was required of him and no more. Most of his work was over six or seven furlongs, when he started behind his companions and moved up to join them over the last two furlongs. They set off at a steady pace, working up to a real good speed over the final stretch. Occasionally, for a change, he jumped off a neck in front and came five furlongs, stepping along all the way. Worked in this way he galloped more freely, and when Dick felt he needed a good blow-out he used this method of achieving it.

Throughout, he took his work with complete calm, neither fussing beforehand nor getting stirred up afterwards. The only occasion upon which I can remember him getting on his toes was when, for a change, Dick worked him the reverse way of the trial ground and on the way back, which led along the trial ground, he thought that he was going to come up again the ordinary way. As soon as he had passed the starting point and realised he was on the way home, he lapsed into his customary relaxed state. Long before he got home, he had always dried off completely.

So his preparation continued, and he thrived on it. Always clean winded, he strengthened and muscled up, went better every time he worked and with his gleaming coat, bright eye and easy, swinging step looked the epitome of an equine athlete approaching the peak of condition.

Meanwhile the eyes of the racing public and the critics were upon the horses contesting the warming-up races – 'trials' is hardly the word for them – for the Two Thousand.

The first of these was the Ascot Two Thousand Guineas Trial, seven furlongs, on 3 April. It drew a field of ten and was won comfortably by Good Bond (Majority Blue–Time Honoured, by Supreme Court), a nice-looking colt, half brother to the Grand Prix de Paris winner Roll of Honour (by Miralgo). Good Bond, who was trained by Ryan Price and ridden by the able and artistic Jimmy Lindley, had proved himself a two-year-old of some ability, winning the last three of his five races in 1970, including the Horris Hill Stakes at Newbury, and being given 8 st 12 lb in the Free Handicap.

Next came the Usher Stakes at Kempton on 10 April. The race chosen for My Swallow, it was duly won by him in impeccable style. He beat Ma-Shema, of whom his trainer John Sutcliffe junior had a high regard, and the critics were very impressed. I found no fault in My Swallow's performance or appearance: he won fluently and Paul Davey had him looking a picture; but I was not very impressed by Ma-Shema, who gave me the idea that his trainer might have overrated him. He failed to win that season, though running second, receiving 11 lb, in the Cork and Orrery Stakes to King's Company (King's Troop–Miss Stephen, by Stephen Paul), who previously had beaten Sparkler (Hard Tack–Diamond Spur, by Preciptic), narrowly and possibly luckily, for the Irish Two Thousand. Clearly My Swallow had trained on and was going to prove a formidable opponent at Newmarket.

The Craven Stakes at Newmarket three days later proved another success for Ryan Price's stable. It was won by Levanter (Le Levanstell–Tenebre, by Tenerani), ridden by Tony Murray. A tough, workmanlike, chesnut colt, Levanter had cantered in for his only race, as a two-year-old, the Houghton Stakes at Newmarket, and was reputed to be considered a champion in the making. However he did not live up to expectations, as he was well beaten in the Chester Vase, won by Linden Tree (Crepello–Verbena, by Vimy), who later ran second in the Derby and was retired from racing after declining to jump off with the others in the Irish Sweeps Derby.

Levanter's failure may have been caused partially by some form of unsoundness, since he only ran once more, winning most unimpressively at Goodwood in May. So far as the Brigadier was concerned, Levanter did not come into calculations, as he was taken out of the Two Thousand.

The Thirsk Classic Trial, also, had no eventual bearing on the Two Thousand since the winner, Sparkler (Hard Tack– Diamond Spur, by Preciptic) was not a runner on the day, though he was destined to feature prominently in the Brigadier's racing career later.

This left the Greenham Stakes, in which the star contender was Mill Reef.

My impression of Mill Reef had always been that, all else equal, he was better than My Swallow and that he was the horse whom we had to fear the most. The first time I saw Mill Reef was when he slaughtered his opponents in the Coventry Stakes at Royal Ascot, and though the field proved of no great distinction he won in the style of a really good colt. A typical American-bred, being advanced in development compared with the average European-bred two-year-old, he was neat, smallish, beautifully made and full of quality. He was particularly powerful over his back, loins and quarters, which ran right down into his second thighs, and had a perfect shoulder and a good girth, his weakest point for my book being his forearms, which were not so powerful, proportionately, as his second thighs. But it was in action that Mill Reef was seen at his best; he had a lovely, flowing, easy stride that swept him over the ground in effortless style and, somehow, transformed him into a bigger horse than he was when at rest.

His owner-breeder, Paul Mellon, a personal friend both on the racecourse and in the hunting field, and a fine supporter of English racing, on the flat as well as over jumps, has long been a familiar and popular figure on the Turf in this country.

Our connection with Mill Reef is further strengthened by Jean being a first cousin of the late Peter Hastings-Bass, her mother and Peter's being sisters. Peter trained at Kingsclere till he died at a tragically young age, the property then being inherited by his eldest son, William, whose sister Emma is married to Ian Balding. Further, the three Hastings-Bass boys, William, Simon and John were at Winchester, where our two boys, Ian and Andrew, were also educated.

While a number of winners of the Two Thousand Guineas have taken in the Greenham Stakes as a preliminary, the last horse to be successful in both races was Orwell (Gainsborough–Golden Hair, by Golden Sun). A brilliant two-year-old, who won the Chesham Stakes, the National Breeders Stakes, the Imperial Produce Stakes, Champagne Stakes and Middle Park Stakes, his single defeat that season was in the Great Surrey Foal Plate at Epsom, which probably can be attributed to his having bad knees, which is a grave disadvantage at Epsom.

Orwell failed in the Derby and the St Leger, his only other victory as a three-year-old, apart from the Greenham and Two Thousand, being in the Great Foal Plate (ten furlongs) at Newmarket. He was trained at Manton by Joe Lawson for Mr Washington Singer. Apart from his faulty knees, Orwell had bent, curby hocks, and since he imparted one or both of these weaknesses to many of his progeny it is not surprising that he was a failure at stud.

In recent years Only for Life and Right Tack were both beaten in the Greenham, but went on to win the Two Thousand.

It is not difficult to be influenced by superstition in racing, and Mill Reef's probable, indeed virtually certain, success in the Greenham seemed a good omen for the Brigadier at Newmarket.

Six runners opposed Mill Reef at Newbury, where the going was good and a large crowd had gathered to see the star attraction. Of his rivals, only Breeder's Dream (Tudor Melody–La Duchesse, by Prince Bio), carrying Mr David Robinson's colours, and Swing Easy found any support in the market, being at four to one and six to one, respectively, with Mill Reef a hot favourite at nine to four on.

Ian Balding had Mill Reef looking magnificent, full of muscle, with a bloom on his coat and well forward in condition, but still allowing scope for improvement as a result of the race. Mill Reef's usual jockey Geoff Lewis was in the saddle, Frankie Durr being on Breeder's Dream and Jimmy Lindley on Swing Easy.

The race needs little description: Mill Reef went straight to the front, stayed there and won in a canter by four lengths from Breeder's Dream, Swing Easy being a further three lengths away in third place.

I must admit that this performance gave me cause to think. Clearly Mill Reef had trained on, was really well, was likely to improve a little by Two Thousand day and, unless Breeder's Dream and Swing Easy had deteriorated – both were having their first race of the season – the form was good. This was underlined by Swing Easy finishing seven lengths behind Mill Reef, whereas he was only three lengths behind Brigadier Gerard in the Middle Park Stakes and the same distance behind My Swallow in the Prix de la Salamandre.

It may have been wishful thinking, but Swing Easy gave me the impression that he had not yet come to hand and, in consequence, had run below form. This was supported by the weights of the Two-Year-Old Free Handicap, in which Swing Easy had been rated 1 lb in front of Breeder's Dream.

Taking the Free Handicap as a more accurate assessment of Swing Easy than the Greenham Stakes, Swing Easy came out the same amount behind Mill Reef as he proved to be behind My Swallow as a two-year-old, which on the running of My Swallow against Mill Reef in the Prix Robert Papin was almost exactly correct. On this basis, we were back on square one, with the Brigadier holding the same chance in the Two Thousand as he did before the Greenham was run.

With My Swallow and Mill Reef having won so impressively, few paid any attention to the Brigadier. For the critics and the public, the Two Thousand remained a two-horse race. However at West Ilsley our hopes were in no way shaken, for the Brigadier continued to work magnificently and to look better and better each day. While he had grown in height since he was a two-year-old, he had filled out in proportion, losing the immature look of his earlier juvenile days and presenting an appearance which could not fail to command respect from the most ardent of his rivals' supporters.

He delighted Joe Mercer every time he rode him, thrived on his work and consistently showed his superiority over every horse with which he galloped, regardless of the weights at which they met. He had no difficulty in giving weight and a year to such as Duration, Miracle and Richboy. Since, the previous year, as a three-year-old, Richboy had run second in the Cambridgeshire under 8 st 7 lb, two and a half lengths behind the four-year-old Prince de Galles (9 st 7 lb), who was winning the race for the second year in succession, the Brigadier's home form with him at this stage of the season was no mean feat. Richboy showed that he had retained his ability when at the Newmarket Craven Meeting, he finished a close-up third in the Rubbing House Stakes to Pembroke Castle and Quayside, after being baulked.

We had long ago decided that, as the Brigadier was going to Newmarket without having had a preliminary race, he should have a gallop on a racecourse beforehand. Frank Osgood, manager at Newbury, graciously laid this on for us to take place on the morning of Sunday 18 April, over seven furlongs on the straight course. Jakie Astor kindly gave permission for Grey Sky to work with him, and as Grey Sky had just won the Easter Handicap at Kempton by an easy three lengths under 8 st 13 lb, he was in a position to tell us the time of day.

It was a beautiful, sunny morning when we foregathered at Newbury at 7.30 a.m. Apart from Frank Osgood, his daughter and his groundsmen, and those directly concerned with the Brigadier and the operation, not a soul was about. It was as we wished: quiet, peaceful and private – we were only too pleased for Mill Reef and My Swallow to receive all the publicity.

The horses unboxed, the Brigadier taking a good look round at an environment with which he was already familiar, but in very different circumstances. Though there were no crowds, he realised that something was afoot and his air of expectant alertness showed that his nervous system had awakened to the fact that his long holiday was over and he was on the threshold of a new racing season. With his head up, ears pricked and eyes taking in every detail, he looked the personification of the thoroughbred at his finest.

I have seldom known a horse more observant or interested in everything going on around him; on the downs, he would notice a tractor working two or three miles away. Nothing escaped his eye.

The gallop went smoothly and satisfactorily. Joe tucked him in behind, moved up to join Grey Sky and went easily past him when asked to do so. He pulled up nicely warm but in no way fussed, hardly blew and clearly had enjoyed himself thoroughly.

It was an eminently pleasing outcome to the operation, as we knew that he was thoroughly fit, would come on several pounds as a result of the experience and needed no more than routine work and a final five-furlong pipe-opener to produce him at the peak of condition on the day. Joe Mercer was delighted with the way he went and as we all stood admiring him while he walked round to cool off before being boxed up, we felt confident that he was going to prove very difficult to beat.

The Brigadier's final gallop before the Two Thousand took place on Saturday 24 April, over five furlongs on the trial ground. As usual, Joe rode him, the horses working with him being Duration, to whom he was set to give a year and 15 lb and the three-year-old Magnate, ridden by Bobby Elliott.

The morning could not have been worse. It was blowing a gale, the rain pelted down unceasingly and the sky was black as ink.

We could, of course, have put off the gallop to a later day; but that would have meant altering the timing of the Brigadier's preparation, leaving him wondering why he had been denied his usual Saturday gallop and, perhaps, too fresh, which is when a horse can injure himself through fooling about. Besides, horses sometimes have to race in such conditions, as was the case with the Brigadier in the Champion Stakes of 1971 and the Eclipse Stakes the following season; and if they have not been taught to face rain and wind, they may be disconcerted by it when having to do so. Though, like his dam, the Brigadier detests rain, because both he and La Paiva have exceptionally fine coats, he has never flinched from it. So the gallop went on; indeed, I don't think that it ever occurred to Dick or any of us to consider putting it off.

John Lawrence, now Lord Oaksey, had asked if he could come over to watch the Brigadier's final gallop, but I would not agree, as I felt it unfair to my older friends and colleagues on the Press, such as Roger Mortimer, Frank Byrne and Richard Baerlein of *The Observer* – a newspaper dear to my heart as I had been its racing correspondent for sixteen years – that he should have the sole privilege. In any case, it was an extremely crucial, nerve-wracking affair for me. After months of waiting and having staked our financial future and that of our stud on this one horse, my nerves were reaching a tension which was becoming almost unbearable; so that the fewer spectators and distractions there were, the better. I even found a source of irritation in having to wait a few seconds for Sheilah Hern and her mother to get into the Land-Rover, thinking that any delay might not get us to the finishing point on time.

All was well and we got out, standing peering into the misty gloom, with the rain pouring down on us, straining through glasses blurred and distorted, watching for the horses to set off.

When we picked them out, Duration was in front of the Brigadier, Magnate having dropped right out. As they neared us Duration was still ahead, with the Brigadier just behind him, and thus they passed us. My immediate reaction was disappointment, because I knew what the Brigadier could do to Duration in the ordinary course of events; and I ran to meet the horses as they walked back after pulling up, to hear what Joe Mercer had to say. To my relief, he said: 'It was all right. The kid jumped away four or five lengths in front, while I was still three lengths behind Magnate and I didn't want to ask the Brigadier too much in these conditions, but he had plenty in hand at the finish.'

Even allowing for Duration having finished in front of the Brigadier, it was a pretty good gallop, as Duration was receiving 15 lb and a year. Moreover, Duration was a recent winner, giving 13 lb to the second,

Almagest, who later was to become the Brigadier's lead work horse and travelling companion and had finished first in his previous race, but was disqualified.

Furthermore, Joe was wearing a suede leather jacket, which was soaking wet; and when he got back to the yard and took it off, it was so heavy that he put it on the scale and found then he had been carrying 8 lb more than he reckoned. The lad on Duration was wearing a mackintosh windbreaker, which had not absorbed the rain, so the Brigadier's task had been far more formidable than we had realised, as he was attempting to give Duration a year and 23 lb; taking weight-for-age into account, this represented 37 lb.

A few days later Grey Sky won again, giving 21 lb to the second, at Brighton. This confirmed the merit of the Brigadier's gallop with him at Newbury and gave further cause for hope of success in the Two Thousand.

Three Champions Meet

It now only remained to await the day, but I cannot say that the interval was anything but an ordeal. So many mishaps can occur with a race-horse, as when Solar Slipper got cast on the morning of the Derby of 1948, for which he was fancied greatly, and had to be withdrawn. Every time the telephone rang I wondered whether it was Dick Hern, to say that some disaster had overtaken the Brigadier. But all continued well and when I left for Newmarket on the Wednesday, no ill tidings had reached me. I was staying with Jim Joel at Sefton Lodge, as I have the good fortune to do for the Newmarket meetings and Jean was to come for the day of the race, lunching at Sefton Lodge and then going up to the course.

The meeting opened auspiciously, for the One Thousand Guineas was won by our neighbours Vera and Roger Hue-Williams, with their home-bred filly Altesse Royale (Saint Crespin III–Bleu Azur, by Crepello), bred at Woolton Hill, barely a mile from our own stud. This good, courageous and attractive filly, who was mated with Brigadier Gerard in 1973, had run second in the Nell Gwyn Stakes to Super Honey (Tesco Boy–Crystal Honey, by Honeyway), who went on to win the Princess Elizabeth Stakes at Epsom. Having run third earlier in the season in the Ascot One Thousand Guineas Trial, won by the brilliant two-year-old of the previous season, Cawston's Pride (Con Brio–Cawston Tower, by Maharaj Kumar), Super Honey was having her fourth race of the season in The One Thousand, in which Altesse Royale beat her by a length and a half, third place going to my friend Tom Blackwell's filly Catherine Wheel (Roan Rocket–Queen of Arisai, by Persian Gulf), another mare mated with the Brigadier in 1973 and, like him, a descendant of Pretty Polly through Molly Desmond.

Though, as an inmate of Noel Murless's stable, Altesse Royale was certain to have improved since her defeat by Super Honey – since Noel never forces his horses, but instead allows them to come to hand of their own accord – she was allowed to start at 25 to 1. She was ridden by Yves

Saint-Martin, a brilliant and sympathetic rider who must be classed as one of the best jockeys in the world, the Warren Place first rider, Geoff Lewis, being on Lord Howard de Walden's Magic Flute (Tudor Melody–Filigrana, by Niccolo dell'Arca), who started second favourite and eventually finished fourth. The favourite, Cawston's Pride, who failed to stay or to take any real interest in the proceedings, was fifth.

A really good filly, Altesse Royale proceeded to win the Oaks and the Irish Guinness Oaks, after which she retired for the season.

Jakie Astor's The Bugler, behind whom I had ridden the Brigadier before the Middle Park Stakes, finished third in the next race, his first outing of the season, indicating that the stable as a whole was in form.

After racing on Friday I went with Dick and Sheilah Hern to the racecourse stables to see the Brigadier, who had arrived that afternoon. It was a beautiful, sunny evening and when the Brigadier was stripped for our inspection my heart quickened with pride and admiration. He looked absolute perfection and I said to Dick: 'Win, lose or draw, I've never seen a horse better trained in my life; he looks absolutely grand and does you real credit,' which was no more than the bare truth.

The Brigadier had travelled without turning a hair, knew exactly where he was and why he had come there. Like a general in command of a thoroughly trained, efficient and formidable army, whose morale was at its peak, with a well-laid battle plan at his finger tips, he seemed to be awaiting with eager but calm assurance the outcome of the morrow.

All my friends on the Press seemed unchanged in their view that the Two Thousand was going to be a two-horse race; they were divided in opinion more or less equally between Mill Reef and My Swallow to the exclusion of all other competitors. To those I ran into at Newmarket I told the strength of Brigadier Gerard's home work, but all except one were uninfluenced by this information, doubtless believing Mill Reef and My Swallow capable of putting up the same or better performances. The single exception was Clive Graham of the *Daily Express*, who listened attentively to all I recounted and became the only journalist in the national Press to select the Brigadier and, furthermore, napped him.

The conditions on the first two days of the meeting had been perfect for the Brigadier, the weather warm and the going fast; happily, there was no change before the Two Thousand. This in itself was a good omen.

As is usual with Dick Hern's runners, the Brigadier was led out for a walk at 7.30 a.m. He was as composed and nonchalant as when I had seen him the previous evening, having eaten every scrap of his evening meal and rested well. Of all involved in the operation, he was the least concerned.

The morning passed, spent largely in reading the summing up of the various racing writers' opinions on the race – which with the exception of Clive Graham's held out little or no hope of success for the Brigadier – and attempting to do *The Times* crossword, to which my fellow guests Winifred Gladstone and Harvey Solomon, not altogether surprisingly, made the greater contribution.

Jean arrived in good time for lunch, and strengthened by Jim Joel's excellent fare, we set out for the course.

Apart from our deep personal concern in it, I can recall no race for the Two Thousand to arouse so much public interest. For the whole winter the coming battle between Mill Reef and My Swallow had been debated – a godsend to copy-hungry journalists when racing news flagged – additional flavour being given by the presence of an unbeaten colt in Brigadier Gerard, as well as that of Minsky, a full brother to the previous year's Triple Crown winner Nijinsky (Northern Dancer–Flaming Page, by Bull Page) and winner of his two previous races in 1971, the Gladness Stakes and The Tetrarch Stakes, trained in Ireland by Vincent O'Brien and carrying the colours of the late Charles Engelhard, with Lester Piggott in the saddle.

This build-up, helped by fine weather, drew a large crowd, which began to flow towards the Rowley Mile Course long before racing was due to start.

In prudent anticipation of the dense traffic, lunch at Sefton Lodge had been early, and the euphoria of Jim's wine had worn off some time before the Two Thousand was due to be run. In its place, all the tension of the past months returned; I felt my nerves tingling, the muscles of my face tightening and that I could not stand the strain much longer. I envied the icy calm of such as Lord George Bentinck, who could watch one of his horses go out for a classic, having wagered on it a sum that made the value of the prize insignificant, without a twitch or a tremor.

The race before the Two Thousand was an apprentices' handicap, in which Duration was a runner. He was ridden by one of Dick's boys, L. Davies, and carried 8 st 4 lb. Among his opponents was Mill Reef's chief working companion, National Park, to whom Duration was set to give 6 lb, the field comprising sixteen runners. Had the Kingsclere and West Ilsley stables known the strength of each other's home gallops, they would have seen the writing on the wall, for Duration left the opposition standing to win by five lengths from Water Rat, with National Park a further two and a half lengths away in third place.

We did not appreciate the full impact of this race until some time later, when Jean and I were talking to Ian Balding over a drink after the Champagne Stakes at Salisbury, where both Mill Reef and Brigadier Gerard had won as two-year-olds. Ian said to us:

After the Greenham, I did not think that any horse could beat Mill Reef at a mile and could not believe the result of the Guineas, until I talked to Joe Mercer and he told me how Brigadier Gerard had been galloped before the race. Mill Reef could not have done that. Though National Park is a slightly better horse at home than he is on the racecourse, Mill Reef could never give him that weight.

This candid statement of fact on the part of Mill Reef's trainer effectively disposes of the opinion expressed by some critics that Mill Reef did not run up to his true form in the Two Thousand. The reliability of the result is confirmed further by the running of Mill Reef and My Swallow, who finished exactly as they should have done on their form in the Prix Robert Papin, taking into consideration the draw and the circumstances, as already related.

Consequent to seeing Duration past the scales after his victory, and naturally wishing to saddle the Brigadier himself, Dick had little time to spare in performing this task and getting the horse into the main parade ring in good time; and we were still in the saddling box when an official banged on the door, warning us to hurry up. During the whole operation the Brigadier remained quite unmoved. He stood like a statue, head high, ears pricked, listening attentively to the sounds emanating from without.

When he came into the ring, most of his five opponents, including Mill Reef and My Swallow, were already walking round. The remaining two runners were Good Bond, winner of the Ascot Two Thousand Guineas Trial, ridden by Jimmy Lindley and Brian Taylor's mount, Indian Ruler, an American-bred colt who had won impressively at Newmarket the previous autumn, but had run without distinction behind Good Bond at Ascot and never won another race. The field was the smallest since 1888, when Ayrshire (Hampton–Illuminata) beat five opponents, as did Ormonde in 1886, but this in no way diminished public interest in the race, owing to the quality of its chief protagonists, nor betting on the outcome, as there were many prepared to support either Mill Reef or My Swallow, while up to a week or so before the race it was possible to back the Brigadier each way.

By this time there was not a square inch of space around the parade ring and an air of anticipation pervaded the spectators, as they awaited the entrance of the Brigadier, for he had not been seen in public since his victory in the Middle Park Stakes and all were keen to discover how he had developed during the winter.

When the Brigadier appeared, those who had not seen him in the preliminary ring could not but admire and respect him. In looks he stood out from his rivals, the magnificent condition in which Dick Hern had turned him out emphasising his supremacy in this respect. Bigger and more powerful than Mill Reef, he showed finer quality than My Swallow, while compared to him the other three runners looked handicappers, though good individuals by ordinary standards. Several of those who had not considered his chance began to have doubts as to their judgment.

Dick and I joined Buster, the travelling lad, in the ring, where we were able to take careful stock of our two chief opponents, Mill Reef and My Swallow.

To me, Mill Reef looked appreciably lighter than in the Greenham, but fit to run the race of his life, while My Swallow also was trained to the minute.

About a week before the race, Jean said to me: 'If you had to sum up the race in an article, what would you go for? I want an unprejudiced view.' I answered: 'I think we'll win,' giving the reasons for my belief in the Brigadier's superiority over Mill Reef and My Swallow, as expounded earlier; and as I watched him strolling round the ring with casual assurance, and compared him with his rivals, I felt that my forecast was right.

With only six runners, the draw gave no advantage to any particular position. Mill Reef was drawn number one, on the stands side, followed by Good Bond (No. 2), Indian Ruler (No. 3), Brigadier Gerard (No. 4), Minsky (No. 5) and My Swallow (No. 6).

From a tactical aspect, the only complication of the draw was that Mill Reef and My Swallow were on opposite sides of the runners so that, presuming their riders to regard each other as the chief dangers, either Mill Reef would have to move across to join My Swallow, or vice versa, unless the pair converged.

Brigadier Gerard was No. 1 on the card, by virtue of his position in the alphabet, so was due to lead the parade. When he was led out on to the course, he declined to go in front and Jimmy Lindley obligingly took Good Bond ahead. During all his racing career the Brigadier showed his dislike of parades, perhaps deeming them a waste of time in that they delayed getting on with the race, which was the true purpose of his presence. An interesting contradiction to his disinclination to go in front during a parade is that, when he joined Royal Palace at the Egerton Stud and accompanied him for the first time at exercise, he fretted until he was allowed to lead his companion, when he settled down happily ahead of him.

Apart from this, he remained cool and composed, though more on his toes and alert than in the parade ring. When his turn came to canter to the post, he moved down smoothly and powerfully, as did both Mill Reef and My Swallow.

Both before the race and in the parade ring, Dick, Joe and I decided that Joe's tactics must be determined by the way the race was run. We agreed that Mill Reef and My Swallow were likely to draw away from the others after half way and start to battle it out together from about three furlongs from home; and that, should this prove the case, Joe's best plan would be to keep the Brigadier in a handy position behind them until he met the Dip, two furlongs from home, and then to set him alight and go all out for the winning post. If the race were to develop differently, as in the Middle Park when the leaders set no pace from the start, he would have to employ whatever tactics he thought best, according to the circumstances.

The betting was 6 to 4 Mill Reef, who had eased from 5 to 4; 2 to 1 My Swallow, who had opened at 15 to 8; 11 to 2 Brigadier Gerard, whose early quotation was 6 to 1; 15 to 2 Minsky, 16 to 1 Good Bond and 100 to 1 Indian Ruler.

After seeing the Brigadier out of the parade ring, which he left in as leisurely a manner as if he were returning from exercise at home, with Joe riding on a loose rein and kicking him lightly with his heels to make him walk on, Dick and I made our way on to the top of the stands, to find a place from which to see the race. There was no room there whatsoever, so we went out on the roof, which is reserved for officials and certain others whose duties or position entitle them to be there. It was fortunate that we did so, since otherwise it would have been almost impossible for us to have found a place from which to have obtained a good view of the race.

Jean, who had not come into the parade ring, took up a position in front of the stands, finding herself beside Bruce Hobbs. Just above me stood Dreda Tryon, a friend since my pre-war days in Sussex, who noticed a ladybird on her coat and said to me: 'I'll transfer it to you; it'll bring you luck,' putting it on my shoulder where it remained throughout the race.

The afternoon was warm and sunny, which at Newmarket sometimes makes the runners difficult to pick out, because one is looking into the light; but with only six runners there was no problem in sorting them out.

Two minutes after the advertised time of the race, they were off. My Swallow went straight to the front, followed by Mill Reef, who gradually edged over towards him. The Brigadier lay some two or three lengths behind them, between the pair. The remaining three runners had already dropped behind, to all intents and purposes out of the race.

Brigadier Gerard wins the Two Thousand Guineas, 1971, from Mill Reef and My Swallow

My Swallow continued to bowl along in front, his rider Frankie Durr, an experienced jockey, setting a good pace, but not unreasonably strong considering the fast going. To say, as some did, that My Swallow and Mill Reef ran each other into the ground is nonsense; quite apart from the unmerited aspersion this pronouncement casts on the judgment of two such top-class riders as Frankie Durr and Geoff Lewis, the overall time of the race, exactly average, discounts it.

Other apologists for Mill Reef's defeat argued that the pace was not fast enough!

Three furlongs out Mill Reef had moved up to My Swallow and was racing upsides him. Thus Joe had to move the Brigadier towards the stands, so that he could get a clear run on Mill Reef's near side when he made his challenge. The Brigadier was going well, but My Swallow and Mill Reef were still galloping strongly ahead of him, the former holding a slight lead. At that stage most spectators probably thought that the race lay between the two leaders.

Two furlongs out Joe made his effort, pulling his whip out in his right hand and giving the Brigadier a slap. He took three strides to reach full speed, drew up to Mill Reef and My Swallow and then went by them as if they were standing still, more than a furlong and a half from home. Joe never touched him again, but kept his whip swinging in rhythm with the horse's stride. The Brigadier veered away from it, towards the stands rails, which lost him a little ground, but continued to extend his lead till at the post he was three lengths clear of Mill Reef, who worried My Swallow out of second place by three-quarters of a length.

Minsky was a further five lengths away in fourth place, with Indian Ruler and Good Bond tailed off, twelve lengths behind Minsky.

It was the most impressive victory in the Two Thousand since Tudor Minstrel spreadeagled his opponents in 1947; moreover it was gained at the expense of two exceptional colts, without a semblance of a fluke.

Though few can have backed the Brigadier, he received a wonderful reception. He was an English-bred and owned horse, trained in this country and ridden by an English jockey; and the romance of his financially humble background and the risk we had taken in refusing to sell him appealed to the ordinary follower of racing. Moreover, had he been second, the honours of the race would have gone to America, so far as the owner and breeder were concerned; and while no one would grudge success to so sporting and popular an owner as Paul Mellon, an English victory is always more welcome than a foreign one.

As Dick and I made our way to the winner's enclosure, I was summing up the race in my mind, with a view to deciding whether or not to run the Brigadier in the Derby, as I wanted to make the decision public as soon as possible, so that everyone knew exactly how matters stood regarding that race.

Though the Brigadier had won with great ease and had not been tiring at the finish, I felt that his speed had been the predominating factor in his victory, especially as his pedigree was, essentially, that of a mile to ten-furlong horse.

Besides this, he was still immature and a hard race in the Derby might finish him off at this stage of his racing career, as it has done so many Derby contestants in the past, both winners and losers. Always, we had considered the Brigadier as unlikely to reach his best until he was four, and I did not wish to prejudice his future. Furthermore, though he did not become unbalanced during the descent into the Dip, he was seen to much greater advantage as he breasted the rising ground, which was a clear indication that Epsom, with its steep gradients, would be a far from ideal course for him.

Before we reached the winner's enclosure, I said to Dick that I had made up my mind not to run the Brigadier in the Derby and told at least one member of the Press whom we met on the way. Even in the light of the Brigadier's subsequent record I would still make the same decision.

When I broke the news to Joe after the race, he said: 'I'm delighted. The course wouldn't suit him and you might jar him up.'

The Brigadier returned to the winner's enclosure looking as unconcerned as when he went out for the race. He was hardly damp or blowing and his demeanour seemed to suggest surprise that anyone should not take it for granted that he would be in the position of honour.

In the winner's enclosure after the Two Thousand Guineas; Brigadier Gerard and his owners

The whole procedure was almost a blue print of the Middle Park Stakes, except that in the latter race he had gone to the front at an earlier stage.

Of all the racing successes in my life, the Brigadier's victory in the Two Thousand will remain most dear to me, because it meant so much to us at the time, being so much more important than any race we had ever won and putting our stud, our racing activities and our finances on an entirely different plane to that which we had known before.

Paul Mellon, with his usual courtesy, congratulated us as we stood in the unsaddling enclosure; and as we went in to see the run through of the patrol film of the race, he remarked to Jean with a smile, 'I don't think I'm going to enjoy this very much!'

As we made our way through the car park towards my car, a racegoer stopped me to offer his congratulations and exchange a few words. When I rejoined Jean, who had walked on, she said: 'Who was that? He looked very pleased – and rather relieved.' I answered: 'He had every reason to; he's my bank manager.'

12 *Summer Campaign, 1971*

As usual, the Brigadier was quite unmoved as a result of his race.

One of the most telling factors regarding the effect of a race on a horse is the amount of weight he loses between the time he leaves the stable and his return. This may amount to 40 lb or more. Much of it can be accounted for by travelling; for instance, when the Brigadier went to York for the Benson and Hedges Gold Cup he lost 22 lb, whereas Brigade Major, who went purely for the ride, lost only 8 lb less.

One of the salient points of the Brigadier's racing career was the small amount of weight he lost as a result of his races. When he won the Westbury Stakes at Sandown he never lost a pound, which is so unusual that Dick felt that a mistake must have been made in the reading; but when he broke the ten-furlong record at Ascot next time out, in the Prince of Wales's Stakes, and he was weighed extra carefully, again he was found to have lost no weight. As a rule he lost round about 7 lb, which is negligible, and put it back very quickly afterwards.

The next move in the Brigadier's career was to decide his immediate programme. His engagements included the Irish Two Thousand Guineas, exactly a fortnight ahead, and the Lockinge Stakes at Newbury a further week away.

The Irish classic was a certainty for him and, from a short-term, financial aspect it was arguable that it represented a bird in the hand not to be ignored, since it was worth over £12,000 to the winner.

The only two winners of the Two Thousand to contest the Irish equivalent since the war are Right Tack and High Top. Right Tack won it, High Top ran unplaced, but was found to be suffering from a virus so his defeat can be excused. Right Tack went on to win the St James's Palace Stakes, which proved his last success. High Top, who did not win again, never reproduced the sparkle he showed when winning the Two Thousand, though running courageously when narrowly beaten by Sallust (Pall Mall–Bandarilla, by Matador), owned by Sir Michael Sobell and trained by Dick Hern, in the Sussex Stakes at Goodwood and by Lyphard (Northern Dancer–Goofed, by Court Martial) in the Prix Jacques le Marois at Deauville.

Since the Brigadier had a long campaign ahead of him, embracing a further season, it seemed that it was not a sound policy to race him again so soon after his Newmarket victory. Though he won easily, he had a hard race and, apart from his immaturity and long-term programme, there was the journey to Ireland and back.

The Lockinge Stakes at Newbury was a more feasible proposition, but it entailed taking on older horses, and there is a saying on the Turf worth respect: 'Never take on the older horses with a three-year-old before Royal Ascot.' Though there were attractions about the engagement, not the least being that it was at our home meeting and involved no travelling to speak of, we decided against it.

Thus the Brigadier's next objective became the St James's Palace Stakes, run on the Old Mile at Royal Ascot on Tuesday 15 June. This is the traditional race at Royal Ascot for Two Thousand Guineas horses, as evident in the records. Of the post-war colts to win the Guineas, Tudor Minstrel, Palestine, Nearula, Darius and Right Tack also took the St James's Palace Stakes, which was won by the following post-war runners-up in the Two Thousand: Khaled, King's Bench, Tamerlane, Major Portion, Venture VII, Silly Season and Petingo.

The St James's Palace Stakes has also, occasionally, produced a monumental turn-up, as in 1934 when Flamenco (Flamingo–Valescure, by Swynford) carried Lord Rosebery's 'primrose and rose hoops, rose cap' to victory at the expense of the Two Thousand Guineas winner Colombo (Manna–Lady Nairne, by Chaucer), who had started hot favourite for the Derby to finish third to Windsor Lad (Blandford–Resplendent, by By George!) and Easton (Dark Legend–Phaona, by Phalaris); and when, two years later, the Derby winner Mahmoud (Blenheim–Mah Mahal, by Gainsborough) failed behind Rhodes Scholar (Pharos–Book Law, by Buchan). On both occasions the crucial factor was the going, which was heavy. When the time came, a similar disaster almost overtook the Brigadier.

In the meantime, Mill Reef's attention was turned to middle-distance racing, in which metier he won the Derby by a comfortable two lengths from Linden Tree and Irish Ball, who did not have too good a run, which is often the fate of horses ridden by jockeys unfamiliar with the mile-and-a-half course at Epsom and was confirmed when Irish Ball (Baldric II–Irish Lass, by Sayajirao) subsequently won the Irish Sweeps Derby. Going from strength to strength, Mill Reef completed the season in a blaze of glory, taking the Eclipse Stakes, the King George VI and the Queen Elizabeth Stakes, and, finally, the Prix de l'Arc de Triomphe.

My Swallow, on the other hand, did not train on. He was at his peak on the day of the Two Thousand, in which he had a really hard race, and this may have left its mark. Though given a good rest, not appearing again until the Prix de la Porte Maillot, seven furlongs, on 27 June, he was beaten an easy six lengths by Faraway Son (Ambiopoise–Locust Time), who later was destined to suffer a similar fate at the hands of Brigadier Gerard. Brought out eleven days later for the July Cup, My Swallow was sweating and ill at ease, failing by half a length to cope with the challenge of Realm (Princely Gift–Quita II, by Lavandin) and never ran again.

Of the Brigadier's other defeated opponents in the Two Thousand, Minsky went to North America, where he won several races, and Good Bond won the Northern Goldsmiths' Handicap at Newcastle carrying 9 st 8 lb, finished second in the William Hill Gold Cup, beaten by three-quarters of a length by the five-year-old Caius, a good handicapper, at level weights, and was third in the Diomed Stakes at Epsom and in the St James's Palace Stakes. This says something for the form of the Two Thousand Guineas, in which Good Bond had finished over twenty lengths behind the Brigadier.

So far, the Brigadier had raced only on good or firm going, so that we had no idea how he would perform on soft ground. Dick and I were of the opinion that he would not be inconvenienced unduly, basing this on his slight knee action, as opposed to his being a complete daisy cutter; but Lord Carnarvon assured me that both Queen's Hussar and his progeny were a stone better on firm ground than on soft. Time was to prove him right.

Traditionally, the St James's Palace Stakes is the last race on the first day of the Royal Meeting. The Old Mile, on which it takes place, is 'L' shaped, with a good long run to the bend into the straight. It is particularly suited to a small field which, because of its conditions, the St James's Palace invariably attracts, but it provides a fine spectacle, especially for the connoisseur, to whom quality in racing means more than large fields and an open betting market.

According to stable routine, the Brigadier had been led out in the morning and was then sent to Ascot by horse box.

It was an unpleasant, wet day and the going was soft. Roi Soleil (Skymaster–Kessall, by Stephen Paul) opened the proceedings with a victory for France, though English-owned and bred, respectively by Mrs and Mr Riley-Smith. Ridden by Jimmy Lindley, he revelled in the heavy going and won the Queen Anne Stakes for Mick Bartholomew's Chantilly stable. Roi Soleil later finished unplaced to the Brigadier in the Champion Stakes.

After Arthur (Henry the Seventh–Vacillate, by Verso II) had won the Prince of Wales Stakes for Lady Rosebery, trained at Arundel by John Dunlop, Ireland scored in the Queen's Vase with Parnell (St Paddy–Nella, by Nearco), bred and owned by an old friend, Roderic More O'Ferrall, one of the most knowledgeable breeders in the game, who with comparatively limited resources has produced five classic winners since the war. A year later Parnell ran a great race to finish second to the Brigadier in the King George VI and the Queen Elizabeth Stakes.

As the rain continued to descend, the going deteriorated and Lord Carnarvon looked more and more gloomy – not without reason. The West Ilsley stable scored a victory in the Coventry Stakes, the most important race for two-year-olds at the meeting, with Sir Michael Sobell's home-bred colt Sun Prince (Princely Gift–Costa Sola, by Worden II). This was followed by the Ascot Stakes won by Celtic Cone (Celtic Ash–Fircone, by Mossborough), bred and trained for Lady Delamere by Bernard van Cutsem, whom I have known since he was at Cambridge when I was completing my education at Newmarket.

While the Ascot Stakes was being run, Jean and I were watching the Brigadier walking round the upper ring. He was very full of himself, kicking up his heels, which I never remember him doing at Newmarket – perhaps he appreciated the traditional decorum generally associated with the headquarters of the Turf.

In fact, the Brigadier went so far as to disgrace himself by neighing at the Royal carriage horses, which had been brought up preparatory to the journey back to Windsor.

Three opponents faced the Brigadier: Sparkler (Hard Tack–Diamond Spur, by Preciptic), Ballyhot (Ballyciptic–Hot Coral, by The Phoenix) and Good Bond.

A compact, strong, well-made bay colt, Sparkler had, last time out, won the Diomed Stakes from King's Company, by whom he had been narrowly beaten in the Irish Two Thousand Guineas, and Good Bond. Sparkler was trained by Sam Armstrong, a master of the profession who has now handed the reins over to his son Robert, whom he has taken in as a partner. I had the good fortune to ride a lot for Sam in bumper races, with pretty good results, until I retired from race riding. His son-in-law, Lester Piggott, was on Sparkler.

Ballyhot, trained by John Winter for Mr Daniel Prenn, had won his previous race, a maiden at Doncaster, very easily at odds on and was reputed to have considerable ability.

The betting was 11 to 4 on Brigadier Gerard, 3 to 1 Sparkler, 18 to 1 Good Bond and 33 to 1 Ballyhot. The Brigadier was drawn two, with Ballyhot number one on the outside, Sparkler three and Good Bond four.

Dick and I watched the race on the steps of the stand, just above the lawn and almost opposite the winning post. While we were waiting for the 'off', a lady just below us asked me if I was the owner of Brigadier Gerard, introducing herself and her husband as Dame Jean and Air Vice-Marshal Sir Geoffrey Bromet. She had written to us about the Brigadier, being the daughter of Sir Arthur Conan Doyle, to whose pen Brigadier Gerard owes his name. Dame Jean later most kindly sent me Sir Arthur Conan Doyle's autograph and I feel that he would have appreciated the dramatic moments which immediately followed my brief conversation with his daughter.

By now the going was really heavy. In such conditions it sometimes pays to go to the front, dictate the pace and then make the best of your way home while your opponents are floundering about trying to make up the leeway. I turned over in my mind asking Joe to ride the Brigadier this way, but finally decided that it would be better to leave him to work things out according to the way the race was run. As matters turned out, I wished I had kept to my original idea, for these were the very tactics that Lester Piggott employed on Sparkler and he nearly stole the race.

So when the stalls opened, Lester and Sparkler went straight to the front and on to the rails, with Joe and the Brigadier a couple of lengths behind, followed by Ballyhot and Good Bond.

Sparkler was still ahead and going well as they turned into the straight, the Brigadier tracking him, about two lengths back. When he made the bend and was headed for the winning post, Joe eased the Brigadier out from behind Sparkler to make his challenge. No sooner had he done so than the Brigadier struck a patch of false going, floundered, lost the rhythm of his stride and fell back half a dozen lengths. Lester was making the best of his way home and the Brigadier did not look to have a million-to-one chance of catching him. My heart felt like lead and, as we stood together, Dick and I sensed that the Brigadier was about to meet his first defeat.

Several friends who watched from private boxes, much further down the course from where Dick and I stood, told me afterwards that they did not believe that any horse living could have got going again and made up so much lost ground. Joe felt the same and was on the point of accepting the situation, in order to save the horse a punishing race with no hope of victory when, as he said afterwards, 'the horse started to go of his own accord'. Finding his stride, the Brigadier stuck his head out and laid himself down to the task of closing the gap between himself and Sparkler.

Joe Mercer is a magnificent jockey at any time, but in times of stress he is superb and in the St James's Palace Stakes he excelled himself. Keeping the Brigadier perfectly balanced, which was no mean task in such going, he encouraged him with hands, heels and the swing of his whip; he gave him a tap, and when the horse responded did not touch him again, knowing that he was doing his utmost and would only resent further pressure.

Never have I seen a horse battle harder to win; he simply would not accept defeat and with every stride crept nearer and nearer to Sparkler. He got to his quarters about a hundred yards from home, when Lester looked round; till then he must have thought he was coasting home, having taken an earlier glance back and seen the Brigadier's plight. Suddenly he realised that the Brigadier was on him and he gave Sparkler everything he knew in a desperate endeavour to hang on to his lead. But, inexorably, the Brigadier gained on him, drew level twenty-five yards from home and in the last few strides got his head in front. Ten yards past the post he was half a length to the good.

I hardly dared hope he had won, though I felt he might have done so. As Dick and I made our way to meet the Brigadier, several people congratulated us, saying they were sure the Brigadier had won; but only the judge's verdict counts and when the result of the photograph was announced in our favour I was very deeply relieved.

Of all the Brigadier's victories, this was his most gallant, because apart from the physical effort required to cope with the difficulties which he encountered, the demands on his courage and determination seemed insuperable.

There were some who, understandably, expressed the view that he would never get over the race, but such is his constitution and temperament that he came out of his ordeal completely unscathed; indeed, he was so fresh the next day that he had to be ridden out for an hour.

My original intention, based on the supposition that he would have an easy race in the St James's Palace Stakes, which on form appeared certain, was to run the Brigadier in the July Cup, run over six furlongs.

To those accustomed to the stereotyped patterns into which racehorses' careers fall nowadays, this might seem an odd idea; but I have always felt that versatility should be part of the armament of a top-class racehorse and that for horses to be given the chance of exercising it on the racecourse would do much to enliven the sport.

I will always remember the great battle for the July Cup between Lord Ellesmere's unbeaten filly, Tiffin (Tetratema–Dawn Wind, by Dark Ronald) and Royal Minstrel, which would have gone in the latter's favour had the race finished at the top of the hill, as it does now, instead of in the Dip. Royal Minstrel maintained his top-class speed, also winning the Cork and Orrery Stakes, six furlongs, and just failing in the five-furlong Nunthorpe Stakes, despite winning the Eclipse Stakes, one and a quarter miles, and running in the Derby.

Since the Brigadier had never worked beyond seven furlongs and had not raced beyond a mile, I saw no reason why he should have lost his speed and looked forward to his proving it in the July Cup, a race I would very much like to win. However, after his hard struggle in the St James's Palace Stakes, in which he lost 24 lb, we took the Brigadier out of the July Cup, which thus came to rest with Bob Boucher, through Realm.

Instead, we put the Brigadier by for the Sussex Stakes at Goodwood on 28 July.

Goodwood is a beautiful and unusual course, one of its most notable features being Trundle Hill, which rises steeply not long after the winning post and is crowded with spectators; so that a horse who has not raced at Goodwood, when striking the front in the straight, may hesitate when suddenly confronted with this unusual spectacle. Fred Darling told me that he always made a point of cantering his Goodwood runners on the course to accustom them to this feature if they had not raced there before. Taking a leaf out of the notebook of this great trainer, I arranged with Dick to follow this routine with the Brigadier. In consequence, he journeyed to Goodwood overnight, accompanied by The Bugler, and we all met at Goodwood at 7.30 in the morning to see the two horses work.

To me, early morning exercise is one of the most attractive parts of racing; I like that time of the day, with its freshness and quiet, and it offers an aspect of the sport less formal and tense than that of the racecourse itself. I always like to watch a horse in his final gallops before a particular engagement, and if he works on the morning of the race to watch him when possible.

Jean and I were in London on the previous evening, so we left for Goodwood at 5 a.m., getting there in good time.

The day in the racing profession starts early and by 7 a.m. the stables at Goodwood were very much awake, lads and horses coming and going, the canteen open, newspapers being bought and sold and an occasional trainer appearing to look at his horses. The Brigadier went up to the course by horse box, though the journey was within easy walking distance, as Dick considered this method represented less risk.

Accompanied by The Bugler, he walked round the upper paddock, taking in every detail of the new surroundings and clearly full of himself. Buster rode him, being a first-class rider – he had been a successful rider over hurdles – and unlikely to part company if the Brigadier whipped round or 'put one in'. Though on his toes and giving an odd kick, he behaved well. After walking round for half an hour, the two horses went down to the junction of the round course and the straight, cantered steadily back and pulled up at the foot of Trundle Hill. By that time, the Brigadier had taken in everything and doubtless had an accurate, mental sketch map of the area. When they had cooled off, the two horses were boxed up and returned to the stables to relax until the labours of the afternoon.

The exercise proved of considerable value, apart from the original object of acquainting the Brigadier with the aspect of Trundle Hill. As opposed to his rather brash behaviour at Ascot, the Brigadier when he came into the paddock at Goodwood was much quieter. From this we deduced that the operation of cantering him early in the morning had a very salutary effect on his manners in the afternoon, and in future he always had a canter on the morning of his races. It was not that he needed working, but that the fact of being saddled, ridden and having mild exercise seemed to quell any superfluous exuberance, thus reducing the risk of his injuring himself in the paddock through messing about.

After the work, Jean and I went off to change and have breakfast at Burpham with Jane and John Nelson, both friends from my Newmarket days. Dreda and Charlie Tryon were also staying with the Nelsons and we had a restful and enjoyable morning till it was time to go racing.

It was a pleasant day and though the going at Goodwood was soft it was nothing like the morass of Ascot. The stable took the race preceding the Sussex Stakes, the Richmond Stakes for two-year-olds, with Sallust, who won by three lengths from Touch Paper, winner of the Stewards' Cup at Goodwood in 1972.

There were five runners for the Sussex Stakes, the Brigadier; Faraway Son, who last time out had beaten My Swallow at Longchamp; Joshua, winner of his last two races, the Prix Messidor at Saint-Cloud and a race at Chantilly; Ashleigh, easy winner of the Jersey Stakes at Royal Ascot; and King's Company, who had followed up his victory in the Irish Two Thousand by taking the Cork and Orrery Stakes at Ascot.

Brigadier Gerard was favourite at 6 to 4 on, Faraway Son was 5 to 1, Ashleigh 11 to 2, King's Company 8 to 1 and Joshua 12 to 1. Faraway Son, ridden by Yves Saint-Martin, was drawn on the inside, the Brigadier next, then Joshua, Ashleigh and King's Company. A careful study of the form of our opponents revealed one common factor: their best performances had been achieved at seven furlongs rather than a mile. This clearly indicated that their weakness was likely to be lack of stamina and, consequently, since we knew that the Brigadier stayed a mile well, the best policy would be for him to make the running and gallop the opposition into the ground, unless one of the runners was obliging enough to set a really strong pace. I suggested this plan to Dick and Joe, who agreed that it seemed the best and that, circumstances permitting, Joe would put it into operation.

In all his previous races the Brigadier had come from behind, but we knew that he could gallop effectively in front and was happy to do so, having on occasions worked him this way at home, so we had no qualms about this policy failing on the racecourse.

The ability to race equally well in front and from behind is a most valuable weapon to a racehorse, because it makes him independent of a pacemaker and enables his jockey to deal effectively with the situation, however the race is run. Every horse should be taught to go in front at home, with this eventuality in view. Sometimes horses have an innate dislike to going in front, or if they are in the lead will run too free, or curl up as soon as they are tackled; much depends upon the way they are ridden and worked from their early days and their experiences on the racecourse, but by patient handling and intelligent training most horses can be taught what is required of them.

The Sussex Stakes was the Brigadier's seventh race. By this time, the public had grown accustomed to seeing him dropped in behind the leaders from the start and coming to challenge within the last two furlongs; so that when the field left the stalls and Joe immediately took the lead, a gasp of surprise was audible from the crowd. Ashleigh and King's Company followed him, with Faraway Son and Joshua bringing up the rear, but well in touch.

The runners turned into the straight in this order, the Brigadier still moving easily. Three furlongs from home King's Company and Ashleigh began to weaken, while Joshua and Faraway Son improved. Joshua drew up to the Brigadier's quarters and for a moment it looked as if he was going to make a race of it. Then the Brigadier seemed to recharge his lungs and gather himself for his final run, which took a couple of strides.

Brigadier Gerard winning the Sussex Stakes, Goodwood, 1971, from Faraway Son
and Joshua

Having done so, he went away from the opposition as if they were rooted
to the ground, going on to win in a canter with his ears pricked, by five
lengths from Faraway Son, Joshua being two and a half lengths further
back with Ashleigh and King's Company well behind. The crowd began
to cheer as the Brigadier started his run, the applause growing in volume
and enthusiasm as he approached the winning post.

In practically all his races the Brigadier was ridden out virtually to the
end, however easily he was winning. The reason for this was that in this
class of racing a horse must be really extended if he is to reach that acme
of fitness necessary to success in top international competition. With a

horse of the Brigadier's calibre, it is not easy to extend him fully on the home gallops, since it is liable to finish off the horses working with him and to sour the horse himself, or bore him to the extent that he will not exert himself at all. On the racecourse, when he is already keyed up by the spirit of competition, he will extend himself without realising or resenting it.

In the case of horses of international standard it is the greatest mistake, as is often the case, to let them win hard held in preparatory races, since they are not using their heart and lungs to the full capacity and, therefore, are not doing the work necessary to bring them to the pitch of fitness they must have when really tested.

After the Brigadier was beaten at York, I observed to Jean that it would not surprise me if he ran better than he had ever done before, next time, as he had been really stretched that day and would benefit from it. This speculation was borne out in his subsequent race, the Queen Elizabeth II Stakes, in which he smashed the Ascot mile record.

The public love to see a good horse at full stretch, as opposed to winning comparatively narrowly on a tight rein; and when the Brigadier began his finishing run they knew he would go right the way through with it, no matter how easily he was winning and they cheered him home to the finish.

The choice of the Brigadier's next race lay between the Prix Jacques le Marois at Deauville on 8 August, or the Goodwood Mile on 28 August. Financially, the Deauville race was by far the more attractive proposition, being worth some £17,000, while the Goodwood Mile carried a prize of a mere £3,000 odd. But the Goodwood Mile represented a better spacing in time than the Deauville race, being a month after the Sussex Stakes and a month before his following objective, the Queen Elizabeth II Stakes at Ascot. With a top-class horse, it is a wise policy to build his programme round his main engagements, allowing the most desirable intervals between races, rather than be tempted by financially attractive prizes which may throw out the schedule and perhaps take the edge off him for the main objective. Sometimes it is possible to get away with it, but more often than not the policy has unpleasant repercussions.

In the case of American racing, where horses are quartered at racecourses for months at a time and all work is done on the track, the situation is entirely different. There is no travelling and thus horses can be raced more frequently, using engagements on the track instead of preparatory gallops.

Under the English system of racing it is possible to race horses frequently if they have a tough constitution and are good travellers, but not at absolute top level or when they have not reached maturity, without paying for it.

In all probability, we could have taken the Brigadier to Deauville, won the Prix Jacques le Marois and left his future unimpaired, so tough was he, physically and mentally. The form book supports this argument, but it is easy to be wise after the event and, at the time, I felt it more sensible to keep to the policy of dividing his races evenly in time, with about a month in between.

The going for the Goodwood Mile was softer than the Brigadier really liked – *Raceform* described it as 'yielding' – but the opposition was less than formidable. It consisted only of a former opponent in Ashleigh, to whom the Brigadier was giving 5 lb, and the consistent and game four-year-old Gold Rod, from whom the Brigadier received 8 lb. Gold Rod was to oppose the Brigadier in many of his later races, thereby amassing a substantial amount in place money, a policy which owners of useful horses below the top class could do worse than emulate.

The situation was reflected in the betting, which went: 6 to 1 on Brigadier Gerard, 6 to 1 Gold Rod, 14 to 1 Ashleigh. Lester Piggott was on Gold Rod and the Irish jockey C. Roche on Ashleigh.

As anticipated, it proved a bloodless victory: the Brigadier went straight to the front, galloped the other two into the ground and won by ten lengths from Gold Rod, who was three lengths ahead of Ashleigh. Gold Rod next ran at Maisons-Laffitte over ten furlongs, a distance beyond his best, and won by a neck from Amadou, who later in the season finished some twenty lengths behind Brigadier Gerard in the Champion Stakes.

With the Goodwood Mile behind him, the Brigadier was now approaching the end of his three-year-old career, having only two more engagements in the programme mapped out for him. These were the Queen Elizabeth II Stakes at Ascot and the Champion Stakes at Newmarket. The lucrative Prix du Moulin de Longchamp on Arc de Triomphe day and run over a mile lay at the Brigadier's mercy, but it came too soon before the Champion Stakes, as compared with the Queen Elizabeth II Stakes; and since the planning of the Brigadier's four-year-old career depended entirely upon how he coped with the mile and a quarter of the Champion Stakes, it was imperative not only that he ran in this race, but that he was at his best when he contested it. So he was not even entered for the Prix du Moulin.

13 *Autumn Campaign, 1971*

Though he had won the Two Thousand brilliantly, the Brigadier gave me the impression that he was improving as the season advanced. He thrived in the warm weather, reached the peak of his form in midsummer and, as time was to show, was able to maintain it right through to the autumn, even after he had broken in his coat.

The Prix du Moulin, as it turned out, was won by Faraway Son, who beat Gold Rod by half a length at level weights.

The Queen Elizabeth II at Ascot, on the Old Mile, found conditions very different from those which prevailed for the St James's Palace Stakes. The going was firm, the weather fine. As if to make up for the ordeal he had undergone when the Brigadier last visited Ascot, fate decreed that everything should be in his favour. This was so for all his other races at Ascot.

In the Queen Elizabeth II Stakes there were only two runners besides the Brigadier: the persevering Ashleigh from Paddy Prendergast's stable, this time ridden by Lester Piggott and receiving 1 lb from the Brigadier, and the French colt Dictus, a four-year-old who had beaten Sparkler by half a length for the Prix Jacques le Marois at Deauville, with the Queen Anne Stakes winner, Roi Soleil, third. No doubt the connections of Dictus were basing their decision to run against the Brigadier on a literal interpretation of the St James's Palace Stakes form.

We left the tactics to Joe to work out, according to circumstances, as Dictus was a proved miler and there was no point in trying to gallop him into the ground, just for the sake of doing so. Possibly remembering how nearly he had beaten the Brigadier through forceful tactics in the St James's Palace Stakes, Lester Piggott jumped Ashleigh smartly out of the stalls and at once took him into the lead. Joe was content to let the Brigadier follow him for the first four furlongs, after which he went by him hard held, and the race was over. Striding ahead, with his ears pricked, the Brigadier won by eight lengths, Dictus passing Ashleigh in

Brigadier Gerard winning the Queen Elizabeth II Stakes, Ascot, 1971, from Dictus
and Ashleigh

the straight to take second place. This pulverising defeat of Dictus,
following on the result of the Prix Jacques le Marois, established the
Brigadier beyond doubt as by far the best miler in Europe. The next
question was: 'How will he fare over a mile and a quarter?'

My own feeling, also that of Dick Hern and Joe Mercer, was that he was
sure to stay the extra two furlongs. On pedigree, he was a gilt-edged miler
with every chance of staying ten furlongs – had his sire Queen's Hussar
been allowed to race beyond a mile, it would have been far easier to assess
the Brigadier's potential as regards distance, but the ill-balanced and timid
policy by which his four-year-old career was directed left breeders in the
dark as to this factor.

One of the tragedies of modern racing and breeding is that, because of commercialism, the desire to conceal a horse's possible weaknesses is far more evident than the wish to prove his qualities. Thus, all too often, horses are rushed off to stud before they have been tested against those of other generations, over varying distances and as four-year-olds. The more a breeder knows about the stallions he is using, the easier it is to produce good stock and to mate his mares to their best advantage. In the long run, it is better to shun improperly proved sires until they have had, at least, three-year-olds running, unless there is a particular reason for using a new sire. This only applies to breeders who race their own stock; those who breed yearlings for sale need only worry about what will attract buyers, as it is the buyers who will burn their fingers, not the breeder, if the product proves an expensive failure.

Apart from his pedigree, the Brigadier's racing class and his relaxed style of racing favoured the likelihood of a mile and a quarter proving well within his compass.

Though about to be raced over a distance appreciably further than that which he had attempted before, the Brigadier was never galloped beyond a mile. He once cantered ten furlongs very steadily, merely to give him a change, but most of his fast work was over six or seven furlongs.

Despite having been in hard training since March and having had five races against the best horses available to oppose him, the Brigadier continued to work with enthusiasm, improve in looks and put on weight. Undoubtedly, he was better than at the start of the season as, indeed, he should have been, though this is by no means always the case with horses who have been in hard training for so long.

Everything proceeded smoothly and satisfactorily with the Brigadier's preparation, and we felt confident that his final test of the season would prove him well able to stay an extra two furlongs, bringing his unbeaten record up to ten.

The portents were favourable in that the first two days of the meeting were fine and the going good, while on the day before the Champion Stakes Joshua, whom the Brigadier had beaten so far at Goodwood, won the Challenge Stakes by four lengths from Abella, an Irish filly who had previously won at the Curragh by five lengths.

During racing I ran into Phil Bull, one of the best-informed and most intelligent men in racing, our conversation taking the line of the effect of going on a racehorse's form. Phil told me that he had made a very careful study of this factor and had come to the firm conclusion that the predominating influence on a horse's ability to gallop effectively in heavy going was his weight. He had proved this time and time again, on occasions putting it to profitable use when backing horses. He explained that the heavier a horse is, the deeper his feet sink into soft ground, necessitating relatively greater effort to pull them out again than is the case with a light horse. So that a big horse, such as the Brigadier, is at a great disadvantage with a small horse when the going is soft, even more so when it is heavy. He ended by saying: 'Mark my words; be very careful about running your horse when the going is heavy. I know he's won in the soft, but he's twice the horse on top of the ground.' But with the sun shining and the going perfect, it did not seem that his warning was applicable to the Champion Stakes on the morrow. I went to bed with no qualms or thoughts of foreboding. It was as well for the peace of my slumber that I did not know what lay ahead.

When I awoke, the weather had changed. The morning was dull and overcast, with a thin rain falling and my optimism of the previous two days began to dissolve.

Out on the Heath at 7.30 a.m., though the weather was damp and miserable, the going was still pretty good. The Brigadier was walking round with Dick's Cesarewitch runner Biskrah; Buster was leading him and his lad Williamson riding him. He was full of himself, giving a kick every now and then, and I was relieved that Buster had him on the rein, since without this insurance he looked as if he might have unshipped his rider and got loose.

Joe had arranged to ride him, being due to arrive when the Brigadier was ready to canter. The only other owner in sight was Wilfred Sherman, who had a two-year-old, Princely Son, in the first race, whom Joe was going to ride a canter after we had worked the Brigadier, preparatory to partnering him in the afternoon. We stood chatting together, all feeling rather cold and miserable till, in due course, Joe appeared. Buster gave him a leg up, having taken the rein off first – any jockey who gets up before making sure the leading rein has been detached stands the chance of setting off with this appendage trailing behind him, which is not conducive to safety or enjoyment.

The Brigadier and his companion jogged away into the drizzle, turning after four furlongs and cantering back steadily.

Though we did not appreciate it at the time, Biskrah, who had recently won the Ruffold Abbey Handicap at Doncaster on firm ground, was no more at home in soft going than the Brigadier. A particularly fine-looking, rather heavily built individual, owned by Lady Beaverbrook, Biskrah ran disappointingly in the Cesarewitch, but as a four-year-old when trained by Scobie Breasley won three of his five races, including the Goodwood Stakes and the Doncaster Cup, all on firm ground.

Walter Sherman was rewarded for getting up to face the discomforts of the morning, as Princely Son, a neat chestnut colt of quality by Princely Gift, out of the Pinza mare Pinol and trained by Les Hall, gave Joe a comfortable ride to win the first race by five lengths, having been backed down from four to one to favourite at two to one. Had I been interested in betting that day, it would not have been difficult to surmise, at 7.30 a.m., that Princely Son was considerably fancied. But all my thoughts were on the Champion Stakes and, as I returned to breakfast at Sefton Lodge and the rain started to fall more heavily, I began to have considerable misgivings as to what the going would be like by 3.40 p.m.

As before the Two Thousand, Jean lunched at Sefton Lodge; after the happy outcome of the Middle Park Stakes and the Two Thousand, we had grown to feel that Jim Joel's pre-racing hospitality was a passport to victory.

The rain continued unceasingly and it needed all the generosity of the alcoholic side of Jim's lunch to counterbalance the gloom which the weather evoked.

Arriving on the racecourse, one of the first friends I met was John Lawrence. 'Well, what about this?', he said indicating the rain. 'Are you going to run?' I answered, 'Oh yes. Good jumping going and the same for all,' though the light-hearted nature of my reply was more forced than felt, for I was far from happy at the prospect of the Brigadier having his first trial over a mile and a quarter on going which was deteriorating every minute. But I was determined that he should run, not only because this race had been his objective since his victory in the Two Thousand and by shirking the issue we should still be in the dark as to how his four-year-old season should be planned, but because a large crowd had come to Newmarket especially to see him run. Jean went along with me in this policy.

After all, had the Brigadier not run into a patch of false ground in the St James's Palace Stakes he would have beaten Sparkler more easily, and the going at Newmarket could not be worse than it was at Ascot.

Nine horses opposed the Brigadier in the Champion Stakes, the numerical strength of the field doubtless being influenced by the belief held in some quarters that a mile and a quarter would prove beyond him. His rivals were: the French-trained colts, Tratteggio, Roi Soleil and Amadou; Jim Joel's good five-year-old Welsh Pageant, who had beaten Joshua a head for the Hungerford Stakes and finished third to Mill Reef and Caro in the Eclipse Stakes, beaten four lengths and two and a half lengths after being baulked; the gallant Gold Rod; Rarity, an Irish colt from Paddy Prendergast's stable and winner of the Ballymoss Stakes and the Desmond Stakes, in the latter beating the Irish Sweeps Derby second Lombardo; and the outsiders Tamil, Great Wall and Leander.

The Brigadier opened at 15 to 8 on, shortening to 2 to 1 on, there being little favour in the market for any of the other runners. Tratteggio, winner last time out of the Prix Henri Delamarre by six lengths and trained by Alec Head, was second favourite at 17 to 2, followed by Welsh Pageant (9 to 1), Gold Rod (13 to 1), Rarity (20 to 1) and Amadou (25 to 1).

The afternoon dragged on, the rain kept falling, the going became heavier and my depression increased.

As related, Biskrah disappointed the stable in the Cesarewitch, which was won by Orosio (Aureole–Orcara, by Arctic Prince), bred by Phil Bull, whose words kept coming back to me in an uncomfortable manner; it seemed an ominous portent.

During the Cesarewitch I went up to the top ring to see the Brigadier, standing in the shelter of one of the saddling boxes in company with Rarity's trainer, Paddy Prendergast, and Rufus Beasley. Both generously admired the Brigadier, who was his usual composed self, his early morning exercise having rid him of any undesirable exuberance, which a state of over freshness might have induced in him. As always at Newmarket his behaviour was impeccable.

Welsh Pageant looked the best of the other runners, but like the Brigadier, I knew he disliked the soft going, nor was he so good at ten furlongs as at a mile. Besides, we had the beating of him on form, through Joshua. The French horses did not catch the eye, though experience has shown that the paddock neglected sometimes finishes up in the winner's enclosure.

Rarity, whom I had not seen before, was a small, lightly built, bay colt, attractive in a gazelle-like way and very much fitting Phil Bull's blueprint for a soft ground performer. In fact, his form in the soft was extremely good, for Lombardo, whom he had beaten by four lengths in the Desmond Stakes (ten furlongs), had finished second by three lengths in the Irish Sweeps Derby to Irish Ball, who after a bad run had been beaten only four and a half lengths in the Derby, when third to Mill Reef. Moreover, Lombardo was better at a mile and a quarter than a mile and a half, which reflected still more credit on Rarity, who, on the book, could be made out to be only three and a half lengths behind Mill Reef, less if allowance is made for Lombardo being better at ten furlongs than at twelve.

Still, as the Brigadier had beaten Mill Reef by three lengths in the Two

Brigadier Gerard going out for the Champion Stakes, Newmarket, 1971; with
Buster Haslam

Thousand, I felt that even in soft ground there was no horse in the
Champion Stakes capable of beating him. What I failed to appreciate was
the extent to which the going had deteriorated.

We formed no particular riding plans, as Joe knew the Brigadier so well
and the pattern of the race was likely to be shaped automatically by Welsh
Pageant, who was a front runner.

The rain was driving into the horses' faces when they came out on to the
course for the parade, and the Brigadier clearly disliked it intensely. On
the way down to the post, Freddie Head on Tratteggio gave the impres-

sion that he felt that the horse was going to take off with him, as he pulled up almost to a trot. Whereupon the Brigadier, who was close to him, pulled up altogether; but Joe took no notice, coaxing him into a trot and then again into a canter. But some onlookers interpreted his behaviour as a sign that he was getting fed up with racing and might not train on. As the following season was to show, let alone the Champion Stakes itself, this was far from the case; it was the combined influence of Tratteggio slowing up suddenly beside him and his dislike of the long trail down to the post with the rain beating against his face, which caused him to behave thus.

In the poor visibility it was not easy to see the early running clearly, but Welsh Pageant, Gold Rod, Leander and Roi Soleil could be discerned as the leading group, with the Brigadier tucked in close behind them.

Dick and I were standing on the roof, as in the Two Thousand, which may have afforded the best view, though certainly not the driest. Approaching the Bushes, Welsh Pageant was in the lead, with the Brigadier breathing down his neck, Gold Rod handy and Pat Eddery on Rarity steadily making up ground.

The Brigadier was travelling very easily, Joe sitting still on him, awaiting the moment to launch his challenge. As he entered the Dip he let him go and the Brigadier moved smoothly into a lead of some three lengths. 'It's all over,' muttered Dick beside me; but no sooner were the words out of his mouth than it was evident that the Brigadier was not accelerating in his usual manner. Instead of bouncing away with the terrific power his hindquarters produced from the purchase afforded by his action on firm ground, he was plugging along at the same pace, dragging his feet out of the mud into which they were sinking at every stride.

Similarly handicapped, Welsh Pageant was dropping back beaten, but little Rarity was skimming over the soaked ground like a well-cast pebble thrown in ducks-and-drakes, steadily but surely closing the gap, beautifully balanced by Pat Eddery.

I watched as in a nightmare while Rarity drew up to the Brigadier, reaching first his quarters, then his girth, then his shoulders. Joe had sensed the danger as soon as Rarity had reached the Brigadier's quarters and was riding him for all he was worth, at the same time keeping him on an even keel. The Brigadier was doing his utmost, but simply could not peg back Rarity, who drew up to his head in the last fifty yards and, as the challenger able to make good use of the holding turf, seemed sure to win. But, as in the St James's Palace Stakes, the Brigadier's determination and courage proved insuperable. Putting in everything he knew, he kept his head in front to the post.

From where Dick and I stood, just past the post, I was sure that Rarity had won and all the bitterness of defeat came upon me. It was not just that the Brigadier had lost a rich prize and an unbeaten record, but that he had struggled so valiantly and vainly against such odds, in terms of going.

As we left the roof, I said to Dick: 'He's beaten; it was the going I'm afraid, but he's run a great race.' From her position at ground level, at a different angle, Jean thought he had won by at least a neck: I envied her the mental anguish she was saved.

On the way to the unsaddling enclosure, several people to my utter astonishment congratulated us, apparently having no doubt that the Brigadier had won; and when his number went up my relief and joy were unbounded.

Mentally, it had been a worse race for me than the St James's Palace Stakes in the closing stages, but for the Brigadier the latter presented a more severe ordeal; because, not only had he been thrown completely out of his stride when striking the patch of false ground, but he had an almost impossible amount of ground to make up, whereas in the Champion Stakes it was only in the last fifty yards or so that he really had to battle, desperate though the struggle proved to be.

The Champion Stakes left me in no doubt concerning the Brigadier's ability to stay a mile and a quarter. Not only was the going greatly to his disadvantage, but it was equivalent to adding another furlong to the race, so holding had it become. Joe Mercer and Dick held the same opinion. Nevertheless, several critics attributed the narrowness of the Brigadier's victory to failing stamina, rather than the state of the ground, basing this on the apparent ease with which he was winning at a mile and the way in which Rarity gained on him in the final stages. This can be accounted for by Rarity being considerably better at a mile and a quarter than a mile.

The Brigadier had completed his two-year-old season at Newmarket in the autumn, in the Middle Park Stakes, and as a result of his return visit at the end of his second season he must have remembered the sequence of events, for when he got home Dick said to me: 'He knows he's finished racing for the year; you can tell it from his attitude and demeanour.' This is in keeping with his character and behaviour. He is very intelligent and observant, able to grasp any routine quickly and, having done so, remember it, no matter how long the interval between the phases. This trait has been evident in his work, racing and when he retired to stud. Once he understands what is required of him, he carries out the procedure exactly as he should, without any fuss or trouble.

PART THREE

14 *The Brigadier enters his Last Season*

With the racing season over, Jean and I were able to go into the winter in a calmer and less apprehensive state than the year before. Whatever the Brigadier's future, nothing could take away the brilliant record of his first two seasons, during which he was unbeaten in ten races, including the Middle Park Stakes, Two Thousand Guineas, St James's Palace Stakes, Sussex Stakes and Champion Stakes. No English classic winner had remained unbeaten in ten or more races in his first two seasons since Ormonde, who was foaled in 1883 and won thirteen races during this period. Even the great Pretty Polly was beaten as a three-year-old, in the Prix du Conseil Municipal. Unbeaten classic horses are usually found to have been carefully raced, with an eye to maintaining their record, as opposed to finding out how good they are. The triple crown winner Bahram, for instance, had two less races as a three-year-old than Brigadier Gerard and never took on older horses, or raced as a four-year-old. Though I am convinced Bahram was a really good horse, possibly the best I saw before the war, it is not easy to prove it, because the three-year-olds of his generation were a poor lot.

Likewise, only too many classic winners have been retired at the end of their three-year-old season, before they can be found out. Financially, this may be a sound policy and was one which the late Aga Khan followed with his Derby winners Blenheim, Bahram, Mahmoud, My Love and Tulyar. Almost certainly this was good business, since few, if any of them, would have held, let alone increased, their value as four-year-olds.

Recent outstanding classic winners, apart from those such as Crepello and Pinza who broke down, to shirk the issue as four-year-olds are Sea-Bird II, Sir Ivor and Nijinsky.

This policy greatly detracts from the interest of racing and makes it difficult to assess such horses properly as prospective stallions, not only from the aspect of competition with representatives of the next generation, but from that of discovering whether their temperament and

Brigadier Gerard at two years

Brigadier Gerard at three years

Brigadier Gerard at four years

soundness will stand up to three seasons of top-class racing.

We were always determined to race the Brigadier as a four-year-old; in the first place because we were sure he would be relatively better at that age than as a younger horse, and secondly to have the fun of doing so, as it was long odds against our ever owning a horse anywhere near so good. When he was a two-year-old, I even contemplated racing him till he was five, but when he turned out to be so outstanding, it only meant a series of repeat performances, added worry and the loss of a season at stud, when he had already proved himself thoroughly. Had he possessed a staying pedigree, I might have been tempted to aim him at the Ascot Gold Cup as a five-year-old, which the late Lord Derby intended to do with Fairway, had not this brilliant horse developed leg trouble.

The transition from one year to another is always rather an anxious period, especially with fillies from two to three and colts from three to four. The latter sometimes develop ideas more suitable to the purpose of a stallion than a racehorse, or become mulish on the gallops and the racecourse, or bad tempered. Any of these traits can make matters difficult for those who have to train, ride or groom them, with undesirable repercussions in their racing performances.

We did not expect the Brigadier to act in this way, but nothing is entirely predictable in racing, so we could not be sure until his behaviour during the forthcoming off season had revealed itself. As it turned out, his conduct was even more exemplary than during the winter before. He knew exactly what lay ahead and slipped happily back into the familiar routine, enjoying the relaxation from his exertions on the racecourse and the training ground, until the time should come for him to go out to seek further conquests.

Jean and I, as usual, spent the winter at home and hunting with the Beaufort, finding that everyone in the hunt had virtually adopted the Brigadier and followed his career with enthusiastic loyalty. Likewise, throughout the country, he gathered supporters who sent him fan mail, which continued after his retirement.

At the same time, Mill Reef, as his splendid record merited, gathered his supporters and the question arose as to when the two horses would meet and what would be the outcome. It was a situation which was meat and drink for the Press, providing an endless source of copy throughout the winter. Both Paul Mellon and ourselves had announced that, provided circumstances were favourable, we intended to make the Eclipse Stakes at Sandown one of the objectives of our respective horses.

After the Champion Stakes, I had announced to the Press that we would never again ask the Brigadier to race on heavy going, and made it clear that should the ground for the Eclipse be unsuitable he would not run. Despite this, the build-up of 'The Race of the Century' continued, old-timers comparing the situation to the great rivalry of Colorado and Coronach between the two wars. It began when Colorado (Phalaris–Canyon, by Chaucer), owned and bred by the late Lord Derby and trained by George Lambton, slammed Lord Woolavington's home-bred Coronach (Hurry On–Wet Kiss, by Tredennis), trained by Fred Darling, in the Two Thousand Guineas. Colorado was a smallish, strong, neat brown colt and was ridden by Tommy Weston; Coronach was a big rangy chesnut, with a flaxen mane and tail, whose jockey was Joe Childs.

Coronach won the next round, when he ran away with the Derby, in which Colorado was third, Lancegaye separating them. The following year they met again in the Princess of Wales Stakes at Newmarket and the Eclipse Stakes, Colorado winning each time, but as a four-year-old Coronach was not entirely sound in his wind.

Events which are built up by publicity to mammoth proportions seldom realise expectations and often do not take place at all; and many felt, correctly as it turned out, that 'The Race of the Century' would never come off.

On the whole, I am not superstitious, but believe firmly in not courting fate by building horses or races up to a height they may never achieve. In racing there is only one thing that counts: results. When a horse has made his name and finished his career, then is the time to assess and extol him; to do so when he is still racing can end in ignominy or tragedy, typified in the film of Nijinsky, in which the horse's defeats in the Arc de Triomphe and Champion Stakes turned what was intended to be a triumphant epic into a tragedy, as sad and bitter in its end as that of his namesake.

The Eclipse being the Brigadier's main objective, I was keen to give him a preliminary race over the course, especially as Mill Reef had already raced over it when winning the Eclipse in 1971. Though experience of a course such as Sandown may represent only a minor advantage, there is always the possibility that if the race proves a close thing such experience could represent the difference between winning and losing, and I wanted to leave nothing to chance. The plan, therefore, was to bring out the Brigadier in the Coronation Stakes (not to be confused with the Coronation Stakes at Ascot for three-year-old fillies), which is now called the Brigadier Gerard Stakes. This takes place towards the end of April, on the same day as the Whitbread Gold Cup steeplechase, and is run over the same course as the Eclipse. In case this engagement proved impracticable, the Brigadier was also entered in the Westbury Stakes at Sandown, over the identical course, in May.

His provisional programme was the Coronation Stakes at Sandown, the Lockinge Stakes at Newbury, the Prince of Wales Stakes at Royal Ascot, the Eclipse Stakes at Sandown, possibly the King George VI and the Queen Elizabeth Stakes at Ascot, the Benson and Hedges Gold Cup at York and the Champion Stakes. At that stage, we did not view the King George VI and the Queen Elizabeth Stakes as a likely target, and nor did we intend to run him between the Benson and Hedges Gold Cup and the Champion Stakes, in order to give him a rest and to leave the Queen Elizabeth II Stakes open for his stable companion, Sun Prince.

The weather in February was remarkably good for the time of the year and, as a result, horses were forward in their coats. Then it changed, cold bitter winds undoing all the early benefit and playing havoc with training. The Brigadier had done well throughout the winter and continued to thrive, but did not give the impression that he was ready to race; it was evident more in his demeanour than his condition and work, for he looked well and worked pleasingly. However, I was anxious to run him in the Coronation Stakes on 21 April, to give him experience of the course, unless the ground became soft. At the beginning of the week it began to rain and with the approach of the four-day forfeit it looked as if the going might be heavy by the Saturday. Jean was not in favour of running the Brigadier so early, regardless of the going, because of the cold weather and the feeling he gave of not yet being ready to race. As opposed to dilly-dallying until the overnight declaration, leaving the public in the dark until the last moment, we concluded that it would be better to come to a decision before the four-day forfeit stage and, since the weather was still wet, we took him out. No sooner had we done so than a cold wind got up and dried the ground considerably. However, so bleak was the weather on the day that we were not sorry that we had declared forfeit for the Brigadier.

In one respect I was unhappy about the decision, because it meant that instead of having a month between his first two races, he would now have nine days between them, the Lockinge Stakes being on 20 May and the Westbury Stakes on 29 May. Moreover, if he had a hard race in the Lockinge or any form of setback after it, he would miss the chance of a run over the Eclipse Stakes course. The alternative would have been to defer his first appearance of the season to the Westbury Stakes, but I felt that this would be leaving him too long without a race, during which time he might have started to tire of home work. Having brought the Brigadier along gradually, by giving him only four races in his first season and two more in his second, thus building up his confidence, our policy was to give him more racing as a four-year-old, which would entail galloping him less at home.

While, as expounded earlier, it is not difficult to accommodate a three-year-old with galloping companions, because of the scope offered by the weight-for-age scale, it is not so easy to do so in respect of a four-year-old, particularly one of outstanding ability; so that by giving him plenty of racing, home work becomes less of a problem.

At the same time, a horse must have some form of working companion and to fit the bill we bought later in the season from Bill Marshall's stable Almagest, a most attractive little bay five-year-old entire by Star Gazer out of Sovereign Court, by Sovereign Path. He had won several races and had an ideal temperament for the job, being a free runner and willing to go in front. The Brigadier took a tolerant view of Almagest, who led him in all his work, ridden by Bob Asher, a capable and very light rider, and accompanied him everywhere, including the courses at which he raced.

Almagest also did valuable work in making running for the Brigadier in the Queen Elizabeth II Stakes and the Champion Stakes. In this respect it is important to realise that a horse required to make running in top-class races should be an entire, since in most races of this category geldings are ineligible.

Though the Lockinge Stakes was not run until 20 May, the weather was still cold; and when the Brigadier appeared in the preliminary ring he showed his distaste of it by kicking up his heels several times, perhaps to keep warm.

Four opponents faced him in this race over eight furlongs: Gold Rod and Leander, whom he had beaten easily before; Grey Mirage, to whom he was giving 22 lb, impressive winner of Guineas Trials at Kempton and Ascot, also eighth in the Two Thousand; and Crespinall, winner of the Princess Elizabeth Stakes at Epsom. The going was good.

Bearing in mind that we wanted to run the Brigadier nine days later, at Sandown, we agreed that it was not desirable for him to have a harder race than was necessary; so Joe went out with this policy in mind and instructions to ride the race as it came up.

He had no problems. The Brigadier jumped smartly out of the stalls, went into a lead of five lengths after about three furlongs, got rather bored and eased off somewhat so that Joe had to keep him going with his hands, but had two and a half lengths to spare over Grey Mirage at the finish.

It was just the race he required and Joe was delighted with him, which was more than some of the critics were, these apparently expecting to see him win by a furlong; but *Raceform Notebook* observed of it: 'this was a performance of high merit'.

The race took nothing out of the Brigadier and he had only light work before going on to Sandown for the Westbury Stakes. Here, again, the Brigadier's performance did not receive universal acclaim, though he did all that was asked of him.

The Brigadier was set to carry the considerable weight of 9 st 10 lb, against him being Pembroke Castle, Fair World and Juggernaut, each with 9 st, and Ballyhot carrying 8 st 10 lb, all four-year-olds.

As in the Lockinge Stakes, we wanted no more than that he should win without having a hard race, the chief object of the exercise being to give him experience of the Eclipse Stakes course.

To discerning students of form and to the connections of Ballyhot, the

Brigadier was attempting a far more severe task in giving this colt a stone than was realised generally. As *Timeform* pointed out: 'The task that he faced was a tough one and by our reckoning he was no certainty.'

From the start it was a two-horse race. Ballyhot made the running, followed by the Brigadier some two lengths behind him. Joe brought the Brigadier up gradually to join Ballyhot and overhauled him in the last furlong to win by half a length. Though Joe drew his whip and kept it swinging, at no time from the moment that he entered the straight did I feel that the Brigadier would not win. The further he went, the better he went. As in the Lockinge Stakes, it was a workmanlike rather than a spectacular performance, but one in which there was far more merit than most people realised. Before the race, Brian Taylor expressed the view in the jockey's room that the Brigadier could not give a stone to a horse so good as Ballyhot, who had been galloped very well at home. Afterwards he remarked: 'That race may have done Brigadier Gerard a lot of good, but won't have done Ballyhot a lot of good!' His words were prophetic, for Ballyhot did not win again that season, though it is possible that he reacted unfavourably to leaving John Winter and being trained in France, whither he was sent after the Westbury Stakes.

It was a relief to have got these two preliminary races over and, especially, to have been able to give the Brigadier a run over the Eclipse course. As after the Lockinge Stakes, Joe expressed himself well satisfied with the Brigadier's performance and no one was in a better position to express this opinion.

With a view to the long season ahead, the Brigadier had not been tuned right up at home, though he had done plenty of good work, and there was considerable scope for improvement in him. Apart from this, he gave the distinct impression that he had not yet come to hand properly and that a spell of warm weather would see him a very different horse.

On the good military principle of 'know your enemy', Jean and I never kept Mill Reef out of our sights. His first race was to be the Prix Ganay at Longchamp on 30 April, an engagement which at one time we had considered for the Brigadier.

We ruled out sending him for it, because considering the weather we had been having the race came too early; also it would have been a great disappointment to the English racing public for Mill Reef and the Brigadier to have had their first meeting as four-year-olds in France.

Before going to Longchamp, Mill Reef had a public work out at the Newbury Greenham meeting, which took place on 14 and 15 April. When I saw Mill Reef in the paddock he disappointed me: he looked well enough, but not the really outstanding picture of health and well-being that he had presented at the same meeting the previous year, giving me the impression that, if anything, he had lost rather than gained weight since the previous season. I thought that he had grown fractionally during the winter and asked Ian Balding, who was standing beside me, whether this was so. He answered: 'No, he's exactly the same height as he was last year; we're standing a little down hill of him, so he looks a shade taller.'

By contrast, the Brigadier had grown an inch and stood 16.2, being proportionately heavier. Taking a completely unbiased view of the two horses, it did seem to me that the Brigadier had made appreciably the greater improvement from three to four years.

This is understandable, since his bigger frame held more scope for development than that of Mill Reef; besides, like most American-bred horses, Mill Reef had matured earlier than the Brigadier. But putting aside this aspect and assessing Mill Reef purely from the point of view of condition, I felt that he had not thrived as one would have hoped. It must be remembered that with his engagement in the Prix Ganay in mind, Mill Reef had to go into strong work a good deal sooner than the Brigadier, much of his preparation having to take place in cold weather. In these conditions it is not easy to get a horse to do really well, unless he is particularly robust and a good doer; and Mill Reef has always struck me as being a horse who might not be blessed with an iron constitution and insatiable appetite.

He worked pleasingly, though the gallop told no more than that he was happy in himself and moving well, both he and his chief companion in the gallop, Aldie, finishing hard held.

Jean and I went over to Longchamp to see the Prix Ganay and, again, Mill Reef's appearance did not impress me as it did before the Greenham Stakes in 1971; he looked fit to do himself justice, but lighter than I like to see a horse at that point of the season, especially when his chief summer target is in July.

As he cantered down to the post, Jean said to me: 'Do you think he moves quite as well as he did in the Arc de Triomphe?' Mill Reef was such a beautiful and powerful mover that he would fill the eye more than most horses in action, even if he were shin sore or otherwise handicapped; but as I followed him in my glasses to the post, it seemed that, so slightly as to be almost imperceptible, his action was not quite what it was before the Arc de Triomphe.

In the race, Mill Reef performed with majestic authority, leaving the field standing, to win by ten lengths from Amadou.

It was a really impressive performance and the critics went into ecstasies about it. What none of them did was to attempt to evaluate the form. A performance is only as good as the form it represents: if a handicapper beats a selling plater a furlong, it does not make the performance more than a handicap performance, and so on all up the scale. So far as we were concerned, with regard to our prospective meeting with Mill Reef, it was of the greatest importance to find out what the form of the Prix Ganay was really worth. Therefore, after the race and during the weeks that followed, I went into the form of Amadou in detail.

While Amadou had been beaten over twenty lengths by Brigadier Gerard in the Champion Stakes of 1971, in going very unfavourable to the Brigadier, it is probably unfair to assess Amadou on this running, since he might have travelled badly and/or trained off by the time he contested the race.

Before meeting Mill Reef in the Prix Ganay, Amadou had finished fourth to Pistol Packer, Mister Sic Top and Arthur in the Prix d'Harcourt, being beaten a short head by Arthur, from whom he was receiving five pounds. In 1971 Arthur had won the Westbury Stakes at Sandown and the Prince of Wales Stakes at Royal Ascot, but did not distinguish himself when raced in France the following year and was well beaten by Blinis and Lord David after he ran in the Prix d'Harcourt.

Following his second to Mill Reef, Amadou failed to finish in the first ten of twelve runners in the Prix Dollar and was sixth of nine in the Prix Caracalla; so that his form at this period cannot be assessed as anything but moderate, and, consequently, the fact that Mill Reef beat him so easily meant little more than that Mill Reef was in good order.

After the Prix Ganay, Mill Reef had a rest until the Coronation Cup at Epsom on 8 June. He was opposed by Homeric (Ragusa–Darlene, by Dante), a chesnut four-year-old, owned by Sir Michael Sobell and trained by Dick Hern; Wenceslas, a colt of the same age, trained by Vincent O'Brien in Ireland; and his own stable companion, Bright Beam, who for Mill Reef fulfilled the same task as did Almagest later for the Brigadier.

When he appeared in the paddock and his sheet was removed, Mill Reef looked terribly light – when weighed not long afterwards he was found to be nearly 60 lb lighter than he had been as a three-year-old – and I was sure that he was not himself or able to do himself justice.

Of his opponents, Wenceslas had proved quite useful in 1971, but not of much account as a four-year-old; Homeric had run creditably behind Mill Reef in the Derby, in which he became jarred, and was beaten a neck by Athens Wood in the St Leger; in his only previous race in 1972, when rather backward, he had been beaten two lengths by Jim Joel's colt, Selhurst, a half brother by Charlottesville to Royal Palace.

On this form, Mill Reef looked a certainty and the betting reflected it, as he started at fifteen to two on, with Homeric at twelve to one and Wenceslas at fifteen to one.

Bright Beam cut out the work for the first mile, followed by Homeric and Mill Reef. Three furlongs out Joe Mercer shot Homeric past Bright Beam and started to make the best of his way home. Geoff Lewis brought Mill Reef up smoothly to challenge Homeric two furlongs out, but instead of going by him in a few strides, as everyone expected, he took a long time to pass him and had only a neck to spare at the finish. The crowd were dumbfounded and did not know what to make of the result, but the form was franked shortly afterwards at Ascot by Homeric running third to Selhurst and Frascati in the Hardwicke Stakes, being beaten two and a half lengths by Selhurst, half a length more than the distance by which he was beaten by Selhurst when they met previously. Homeric did well later in the season, winning two good races in France and running third in the Prix de l'Arc de Triomphe, despite breaking down, but at that stage of the season he had not come to his best, as the form confirms.

The Coronation Cup proved the last race of Mill Reef's career. He was withdrawn from the Eclipse and later from the Benson and Hedges Gold Cup, because Ian Balding could not get him to his liking; then, finally, came the tragedy of the broken bone in his leg in August, which ended his racing career.

The decision to withdraw Mill Reef at Sandown and York was right: he simply was not his true self at that part of his four-year-old career and should be judged solely on his brilliant record as a three-year-old. At the time of his accident he was doing well and by the rate of his progress he looked set for a second victory in the Prix de l'Arc de Triomphe.

I am glad that Mill Reef and the Brigadier did not meet as four-year-olds, since, in the circumstances, Mill Reef had no chance of winning, and it would have been an unfair contest. As it is, Mill Reef's four-year-old career ended without a defeat and his immortal reputation established the previous year will never be forgotten.

15 *Drama at Royal Ascot and a Wet Eclipse*

The Brigadier's next objective was the Prince of Wales Stakes, ten furlongs at Royal Ascot, and unless the weather intervened or misfortune befell him, he was a certain runner for this race. In the improved weather he thrived and progressed well in his training, and all appeared set for him to bring his unbeaten record up to thirteen, a number which often has proved lucky to me. But on the Sunday before the Royal Ascot meeting events took a dramatic turn.

Joe Mercer was due to fly to Brussels, where he was riding. He emplaned at Newbury, together with the trainer, Bill Marshall and two others. Almost immediately after taking off, the plane hit an overhead cable and crashed into marshy ground. The pilot was killed outright, Marshall was severely injured, Joe being thrown clear. He at once dashed back and pulled Marshall and the other passenger clear just before the plane exploded. It was an act of great heroism, for he came near to losing his life.

Though uninjured, Joe was very badly shaken and suffered severe shock; and the question arose as to whether or not he would be fit enough to ride the Brigadier at Ascot.

No one else had ever ridden the Brigadier in public, and while he was not difficult to ride, it was a partnership which I did not wish to see severed. Apart from Joe knowing the Brigadier inside out and the horse having such confidence in him, it would have been a bitter disappointment to Joe to have had to break the great sequence of unbeaten victories which the pair had built up. From my riding days, I knew how I would have felt in his place. Therefore I insisted that the decision must be entirely with Joe: if he felt he could ride and wanted to do so, he would ride; if he preferred to stand down, Jimmy Lindley would deputise for him.

Those with a purely commercial view of racing – or of any other activity so far as that goes – do not appreciate that one dedicated to his calling can rise above circumstances; that the force of the spirit will often

Brigadier Gerard and Joe Mercer; winning the Prince of Wales Stakes,
Royal Ascot, 1972

overcome physical handicaps; and that determination and courage can
prevail against medical advice. Though a jockey may be sore and shaken,
if his whole being is set on riding a certain horse in a certain race his pain
will be forgotten when he is in the saddle, he will get through the race and,
being a true professional, his performance will be immaculate despite
everything. Moreover, if his horse is one who knows him well, he will
understand and will make the ride easy for him. The late George Duller,
one of the greatest hurdle race riders of all time, once told me that Trespasser, probably the best hurdler in racing history, who was never beaten

and whom he always partnered, used to pull hard and hit his hurdles; but on one occasion when George had broken his ribs and was in considerable pain, Trespasser realised it, never pulled and, by jumping every hurdle clean, avoided jarring him.

By the time Royal Ascot came round, the Brigadier was in splendid trim and conditions were to his liking.

His race was the second of the meeting and six horses opposed him. These were the two five-year-olds, Prominent and Pembroke Castle; Lord David, a four-year-old; and the three-year-olds Steel Pulse, The Broker and Pardner. Prominent had won five consecutive races in 1971, including the P.T.S. Laurels Handicap at Goodwood under 8 st 12 lb, and in his next race after the Prince of Wales Stakes took the £5,000 John Smith Magnet Cup at York under 9 st 4 lb; Pembroke Castle, who had run third to the Brigadier and Ballyhot in the Westbury Stakes, had won three of his five races in 1971, finishing second in the other two; Lord David had won the Rosebery Stakes at Kempton in 1972, carrying 9 st 1 lb, and the Rubbing House Stakes at Newmarket; and Steel Pulse, rated second in the French Free Handicap for two-year-olds in 1971 (one pound below the 1972 French Derby winner Hard to Beat and one pound above Riverman, who was unbeaten in France in 1972) and fourth in the English equivalent, had finished equal fourth in the Two Thousand.

Brigadier Gerard was at two to one on in the betting; second favourite was Lord David, receiving six pounds from the Brigadier. Staff Ingham, trainer of Lord David, held him in high regard and, ridden by Lester Piggott, Lord David was backed from ten to one to eleven to two. Steel Pulse was at tens and there was little or no money for any of the others.

Having had his usual pre-race hack canter in the morning, before leaving home, the Brigadier was on his best behaviour. The carriage horses had not yet appeared, preparatory to their homeward journey, to distract him and his mind was on the task at hand, with no heed to affairs outside the parade ring. When he came to walk down from the top ring to the main ring, between the rows of onlookers, he stood stock still with his head up, gazing ahead as if reading the prices on the Tote indicator. A lad kindly gave him a lead with a horse who had just run in the first race: it was the winner, his old rival Sparkler.

As a younger horse, he would sometimes have a small jump and kick as he came out onto the course to go down to the post, but in maturity he considered himself above such frivolities, sauntering out as if about to take a parade. It was his third visit to Ascot, where before he had encountered sunshine and rain, mud and sound turf, the gruelling test of

Head of the Brigadier after his 13th victory

a battle won against seemingly insuperable odds and the ease of victory, but never the taste of defeat; and he was confident and at ease.

We left Joe to ride his own race, the only proviso being that he should be on the heels of the leader turning into the straight.

When the Ascot course was altered after the war, the straight was shortened by about eighty yards. This changed the whole tactical aspect. Whereas formerly a jockey could turn into the straight knowing he had plenty of time at his disposal before making his challenge, now he must be well there taking the final bend, as is also the case at Longchamp, or he may not catch the leaders. Riding on the old course, I remember once having to grab hold of my horse and hook him behind the leader after making the final bend, in case he hit the front too soon, but for which he would have been beaten; as it was, he won by a head. Similar tactics nowadays would probably end in the leaders getting first run and failure to catch them.

Prominent made the running into the straight, with the Brigadier a length or two behind in second place and Steel Pulse, ridden by Eric Eldin, third.

Two furlongs from home, Joe gave the Brigadier a backhander and he shot forward like a rocket, leaving the field trailing behind, and passed the post five lengths ahead of Steel Pulse, beating the course record.

While the horses were waiting to enter the stalls, the starter said to Joe: 'How are you feeling?' Joe replied: 'I'm feeling fine now, but I won't be in five minutes' time.' As he rode in it was evident that his forecast had been only too right: he was on the verge of collapse, though he had given no sign of it during the race. Afterwards he said: 'The Brigadier knew I wasn't right; he did it all for me and never pulled at all'; and at this stage of his career he had become a very powerful horse and took a strong hold. Joe was unable to ride again at the meeting, Jimmy Lindley deputising for him and winning the St James's Palace Stakes on Sun Prince.

It was a brilliant performance, confirmed when, next time out, Steel Pulse (Diatome–Rachel, by Tudor Minstrel), bred in Sussex by Eric Covell, for whom many years ago I had ridden in point-to-points, won the Irish Sweeps Derby, trained by Scobie Breasley and ridden by Bill Williamson. Of the fourteen runners in this race, the Derby winner Roberto finished twelfth.

We then awaited the momentous confrontation in the Eclipse Stakes nineteen days ahead with Mill Reef, who at this stage was still a probable runner.

As the Brigadier had run three times since the season began, all within a month, he needed no more than routine work to keep him right for the impending battle. He did well on this preparation and we only hoped that the weather would remain favourable, so that the going would be to the liking both of Mill Reef and the Brigadier, producing a fair result, which I was confident would come out in our favour, basing this upon what I had seen of Mill Reef and the evaluation which a careful study of the form in the Prix Ganay had revealed.

Once more, we reiterated that if the going became soft the Brigadier would not run.

A few days before the Eclipse it was announced that Mill Reef would not be in the field, but that it was hoped to have him right for the Benson and Hedges Gold Cup at York on 15 August. The news created something of an anti-climax, in that the Eclipse now looked little more than a walk-over for the Brigadier, a situation that in racing should always be viewed with caution, for on the Turf the unforeseen is the predominating factor, a precept we were fated to experience in the not too distant future.

On the preceding day the going at Sandown was good and the weather dry. Then it began to rain, lightly but relentlessly. And it went on raining.

Jean and I left early for Sandown, as I had arranged to meet Dick there before racing to examine the state of the ground and make a final decision on running.

As we drove towards Esher the rain continued and the day became darker and gloomier. We were determined to run the Brigadier if possible, since the Eclipse was his chief summer target – the King George VI and the Queen Elizabeth Stakes then was not a firm objective – but after the lessons of the past it became clearer with every mile that the decision was going to be a difficult one.

Though the opposition was weak, to run the Brigadier in heavy going was equivalent to putting at least an extra stone on his back. On Admiral Rous's theory that 'a stone will alter any verdict', this was playing with fire, however poor the quality of the opposition; and though by the measure of the Brigadier they were moderate, by average standards they were useful horses. The probable runners were Lord David and Gold Rod, whom the Brigadier had already met and beaten; Charladouce, a winner and placed twice earlier in the season and a winner at Deauville the previous year; Alonso, third at Royal Ascot in the Jersey Stakes on his last appearance; and Home Guard, easy winner of The Tetrarch Stakes in Ireland earlier in the year.

However, as the going had been good the previous day, on the firm rather than the soft side, I was hopeful that it would justify our running.

The Brigadier and Joe Mercer; an informal study at West Ilsley Stables

On arriving at Sandown I went out on to the course and down to the turn into the straight. At some time or other, I have walked every foot of every course over which the Brigadier has raced, and had covered the ten furlongs of the Eclipse Stakes before the Westbury Stakes.

Walking the course is time and effort well spent, since it sometimes reveals a tactical factor of importance; and though my feet became soaked in the process and I got generally wetter, the reconnaissance proved worth while. I discovered, first, that the ground was good enough to merit our taking a calculated risk and running and, second, that the going was markedly faster up the middle of the straight than on or near the rails.

On my way back I met Dick coming up the course towards me and we stopped to discuss the situation. We agreed that the Brigadier would run, and to instruct Joe to pull well out from the rails after making the turn into the straight, come up the middle of the course and not give him a harder race than he could help.

It was noon then and the Eclipse was not due to be run until 2.55; meanwhile the rain kept on and the going steadily deteriorated until by the time of the race it was soft.

Probably on account of his narrow victories in heavy going in the St James's Palace Stakes and the Champion Stakes, punters were wary of backing the Brigadier; at any rate, the price of 11 to 4 on seemed generous, as he opened at 6 to 1 on. Next in the betting came Home Guard and Lord David at 8 to 1, with Alonso at 12 to 1, Charladouce at 40 to 1 and Gold Rod at the somewhat surprising odds of 50 to 1.

When he came into the paddock, the Brigadier showed that he in no way had got over his dislike of the rain, by laying his ears against it as he walked round. He went to the post philosophically, as if conscious that he had an unpleasant rather than difficult task ahead of him and that he would make the best of it, however distasteful he might find it.

Charladouce with Brian Taylor riding made the running, followed by Willie Carson on Gold Rod then the Brigadier, Lord David, Home Guard and Alonso, in that order.

After a mile Charladouce dropped right out and the Brigadier took over as Gold Rod weakened. Lord David moved up to challenge and for a few strides looked as if he was going to put up a fight, but quickly faded out and Gold Rod came on again.

Meanwhile the Brigadier was slogging ahead through the mud and the wet, his tongue out and the rain beating into his face. Joe Mercer did no more than keep him going and he stayed on resolutely to pass the post a length ahead of Gold Rod, with Home Guard, whom Lester Piggott had

Brigadier Gerard winning the Eclipse Stakes, Sandown 1972, from Gold Rod and Home Guard in mud and rain

held up for a late run, third. It was what we expected in the circumstances and to have got through the race successfully was a relief, as there was always the possibility of having asked the Brigadier to face the condition he so loathed once too often; but again he did not let us down. When he returned to the winner's enclosure he seemed really pleased with himself, as if to say: 'You see, I've done it in spite of the mud and rain; comfortably, too.' As usual, he got a warm reception, this time as much for rising above the weather and the going as for winning, and as an appreciation of his presence in the race at all, but for which the large crowd would have seen a sub-standard Eclipse in damp and dismal conditions.

That the race took nothing out of the Brigadier was proved by his having lost only eight pounds.

16 *The Brigadier faces his Greatest Exploit*

For some time we had been considering the possibility of running the Brigadier in the King George VI and the Queen Elizabeth Stakes, and when Mill Reef was announced a non-runner in the Eclipse Stakes we decided that this race would be a stepping-stone towards the more important and greater prize, at Ascot. We kept quiet about the plan, as we wanted to get the Eclipse Stakes safely over before we made any announcement about the Ascot race.

By now the Brigadier had been undefeated in fourteen starts, two less than the unbeaten record established by Ribot, in whose case several victories were achieved in Italy against local opposition of no great quality, whereas every race contested by the Brigadier was the feature of the day.

Though Mill Reef was not to be in the field, the opposition included some of the best middle-distance horses in Europe, whose riders were certain to ensure that the race was run from start to finish, in order to test the Brigadier's stamina to the utmost. This was the crucial point of the venture since the Brigadier would be racing for the first time over a mile and a half, a distance beyond the expectation suggested by his pedigree.

Thus there was a grave chance that the Brigadier might meet his first defeat. But I have always contended that owners in this country place too much emphasis on defeat and not enough on proving horses thoroughly; and that to be beaten honourably carries more merit than preserving an undefeated record by avoiding the issue. Having expounded this theory forcibly and frequently as a journalist, it would have amounted to flouting my own principles if, when faced with the opportunity, I did not put them into practice.

Therefore we decided that the Brigadier would take his chance, win, lose or draw; and we knew that whatever the outcome he would emerge with credit.

In accordance with his usual practice, Dick did not alter his method of training the Brigadier, despite the fact that he was going to race over a longer distance, keeping him to work around seven furlongs. He blossomed in the warm weather, worked with zest and when he left for Ascot I think he was better than he had ever been in his life.

A vital aspect of the race was that of riding tactics. As explained earlier, Ascot is a tricky course in that it is essential, in nine cases out of ten, to be on the heels of the leaders turning into the straight. This makes it dangerous to hold a horse up for a late run or come from some way back, though such tactics are usually favourable to horses of doubtful stamina.

We resolved that the best plan would be for Joe to ride the Brigadier on the assumption that he stayed the distance, relying on his class to enable him to be immediately behind the leaders turning into the straight while still on the bit and open up a lead of a couple of lengths or so, hoping that the momentum of his finishing run, together with his courage, would carry him past the post before his opponents could get to him. The fact that the final twenty yards or so are slightly downhill would help him if his stamina was beginning to give out towards the end.

The day, Saturday 22 July, was fine after some overnight rain and the going officially described as good.

The field was one of the best ever to contest the race, since it included no less than five classic winners, from England, France, Ireland and Italy.

The runners in their order on the racecard were Brigadier Gerard (Joe Mercer) drawn No. 1 on the extreme outside, Fair World (Frankie Durr) drawn No. 4, Parnell (Willie Carson) drawn No. 3, Selhurst (Geoff Lewis) drawn No. 5, Bog Road (Jimmy Lindley) drawn No. 6, Gay Lussac (Lester Piggott) drawn No. 8, Riverman (Freddie Head) drawn No. 7, Steel Pulse (Bill Williamson) drawn No. 9 and Sukawa (Yves Saint-Martin) drawn No. 2.

I was particularly interested to see the French colt Riverman and the unbeaten Italian Derby winner Gay Lussac, on neither of whom I had set eyes before. Riverman, the best horse in France up to ten furlongs, was a sturdy, handsome, medium-sized brown colt by Mill Reef's sire, Never Bend, and was turned out with the customary Alec Head polish. A good looker, he had not quite the best of forelegs and knees, nor the scope of the Brigadier. On his pedigree I doubted his staying a mile and a half, though the same might have been said of the Brigadier.

Gay Lussac was a rangy, lanky chestnut, with an honest head, biggish ears and very clean limbs. He was a shade long in the back and had a fair amount of daylight under him, but looked extremely well and a racehorse of class. Despite his being closely inbred to Nasrullah, he bore no resemblance to the latter whatsoever. Lester Piggott, who was on Gay Lussac, had been over to Italy to ride him work and was reported to have been deeply impressed with the gallop he put up. By Fabergé II out of a mare by Red God, Gay Lussac could not be said to have a mile-and-a-half pedigree and probably won at this distance on his class rather than through genuine stamina.

Steel Pulse and Parnell both looked the part. Steel Pulse, despite his worthy success in the Irish Sweeps Derby, had five lengths and an additional four pounds to make up on the Brigadier on their running in the Prince of Wales Stakes. Parnell, a neat, attractive, chesnut – 'He's never heard of Brigadier Gerard', his lad quipped to me as he passed – had won the Prix Jean Prat and run second to Rock Roi in the Prix du Cadran (the French equivalent of the Ascot Gold Cup); whatever he did, he would not fail through lack of stamina and was turned out by Bernard van Cutsem looking really well. But none, either in looks or condition, surpassed the Brigadier.

He was never any trouble to saddle, his only peculiarity being that he disliked the sponge being thrust into his mouth when it was washed out; so Buster used to encourage him to play with it and thus persuade him to tolerate the operation.

Though the day was hot, the Brigadier was as cool as ice, his immaculate appearance causing him to harden in the betting from 11 to 8 on to 13 to 8 on. Had the race been ten furlongs or a mile, this would have been a remarkably generous price, but the fact that he had never run beyond ten furlongs and was going to have his stamina tested to the full accounted for the bookmakers' apparent magnanimity. Next in the betting was the Italian colt, Gay Lussac, at fives, then Riverman at 17 to 2, Selhurst at 12 to 1, Steel Pulse at 14 to 1, Parnell and the French outsider, Sukawa, at 28 to 1, and the remaining two, Fair World and Bog Road, 66 to 1.

I was not sorry that the Brigadier had been drawn on the outside, as it would ensure him being free of interference in the first furlong or so and enable Joe to sort out his position as he wanted during the early stages of the race. While it was important that the Brigadier was on the heels of the leaders turning into the straight, it was equally important for Joe not to make too much use of him in the first six furlongs, so that he had as much reserve as possible for the final battle.

The pattern of the race developed exactly as we had hoped, apart from the fast pace throughout, which was not to the Brigadier's advantage but was an eventuality we had accepted as inevitable.

Selhurst was the first to show in front and in Jim Joel's famous and distinctive 'black, scarlet cap', held the lead for the first five furlongs. Bunched behind him were Parnell, Sukawa, Gay Lussac and Steel Pulse. The Brigadier was among the last group, but there was not a great deal spanning the whole field at that stage. He was moving very easily, with a clear run on the outside available to him. In this position Joe had all his chief rivals under his eye and could make an instant appreciation of whatever tactical situation developed.

After five furlongs Willie Carson drove Parnell into the lead, keeping him going vigorously to make the utmost use of his stamina.

From half way the Brigadier began to improve his position until in no time, it seemed, he was in second place behind Parnell as they came into the final bend.

So impressively had the manoeuvre been carried out that from this moment Dick and I, who were standing together on the owners' and trainers' stand, felt that the Brigadier was sure to win. Though Parnell was still galloping strongly and could be relied on to keep going to the end, he

Brigadier Gerard winning the Queen Elizabeth II Stakes, Ascot, 1972, in record time

did not possess the Brigadier's devastating speed and ability to quicken; and since Joe as yet had been required to do no more than sit still, he would be able to use the Brigadier's most formidable armament with effect.

After turning into the straight, the Brigadier had two lengths to make up and set about it with his wonted determination. It took him a furlong to catch and master Parnell, who showed no sign of stopping but had not the speed to cope with the Brigadier's challenge.

As the Brigadier gained the lead, the cheering of the vast crowd grew in volume and intensity to a roar such as can seldom have been heard over Ascot Heath. Having struck the front he veered towards the rails, prob-ably wishing to race along them as he liked to do. At the same time, Parnell hung towards the centre of the course. Once in command, the Brigadier was never in danger of being caught and passed the post with a length and a half to spare.

Riverman came from a long way back to take third place, five lengths behind Parnell, then Steel Pulse and Gay Lussac. Thus the five classic winners in the race took the first five places. The time, 2m 32.91s, was only .37s slower than that taken in 1971 by Mill Reef, who as a three-year-old carried a stone less.

It was a thoroughly English victory from a truly international field and the Brigadier was given a tremendous ovation as he returned to the winner's enclosure. But hardly had the applause died down than it was announced that there was a stewards' enquiry. Since Parnell and the Brigadier had changed places in the straight, this was understandable; however, as the Brigadier had won on merit and, so far as I could discern and on Joe Mercer's opinion, Parnell had suffered no interference, I was not unduly perturbed at the announcement. But as the minutes went by and no verdict was given out, I began to grow anxious, fearing that the patrol camera might have revealed something against the Brigadier which I had not noticed.

To escape the crowd of journalists and others who had gathered outside the weighing room, and in order to endure the suspense in cooler and calmer surroundings, I went into the weighing room and found myself standing next to Seamus McGrath, owner-trainer of Bog Road, winner of the Gallinule Stakes earlier in the season but unsuited to the fast ground at Ascot. We stood chatting about the race and one thing and another, which helped to ease the mounting tension; eventually an official gave me the glad news that all was well, the placings remaining unaltered.

Though the Brigadier had edged in the direction of the far rails, the patrol camera revealed that Parnell had been left plenty of room to come

Dick Hern, his trainer, watching the Brigadier being unsaddled after the King George VI and the Queen Elizabeth Stakes

through, if he had been able to do so; also that Parnell himself had come off a true line, veering towards the centre of the course. A point of interest is that one of the French stewards' secretaries, who was present, expressed the opinion that the Brigadier would still have kept the race had it been in France, where the rule governing interference is much stricter than it is in England.

The Brigadier's victory in the King George VI and the Queen

Elizabeth Stakes put the mark of indisputable greatness on him as a race-horse. He had now proved his supremacy from five furlongs to one and a half miles, had beaten the best horses in Europe and, like his famous ancestor Fairway, had won in the topmost class at a distance beyond the expectation of his pedigree.

Standing in the winner's enclosure, a fitting tribute to his merit and courage, he was flawless in his beauty. Bred in England in the face of competition against all the wealth and resources of the foremost studs in America and Europe, he embodied that fusion of the best qualities of a racehorse only to be found in a champion of champions. Though in law he belonged to Jean and to me, in spirit he belonged to England: to all who stood in admiration around him, to the thousands who followed his career and had never seen him, even to those ignorant of his name. In him every Englishman justly could take an equal pride, for he was part of our heritage, evolved from three hundred years of thought and endeavour by those dedicated to perfecting the breed of the racehorse. As I watched him walk away, my heart full of gratitude and joy, I felt – more than pride of achievement – the humility and awe of one chosen by fate to cause this, perhaps the best English racehorse of the century, to be brought into the world and to have in my hand the power to direct his future.

At this moment of his career the Brigadier stood at a pinnacle of achievement unsurpassed by any English racehorse of my time. Indeed only the Italian champion, Ribot, had beaten, by one, his record of fifteen wins in fifteen runs. Apart from lowering Ribot's record and winning the Prix de l'Arc de Triomphe there was little he could do to add to his fame.

Though entered for the Arc de Triomphe, the Brigadier's ultimate target had always been a second Champion Stakes rather than the French race. The reason for this, besides wanting to win the Champion Stakes twice, which no classic winner had done since Fairway in 1928 and 1929, was that most years the Prix de l'Arc de Triomphe is run in soft or heavy going, entirely unsuited to the Brigadier; and even if the ground happened to be favourable overnight, it could easily change adversely by the time the race came to be run, the penalty for withdrawal being ferocious – about £10,000 – owing to the effect on the tiercé betting.

Added to this, we wanted the Brigadier's final race to be in England, where the public who had supported him so faithfully throughout his career could see him make his last appearance on a racecourse.

Had it been our objective to capitalise the Brigadier in the open inter-national market, it would have been a propitious moment to retire him, for his value knew no ceiling. However, since only twenty-four shares were being disposed of, all to private breeders, this aspect did not arise; and since the Brigadier was sound and at the top of his form, we determined to let him soldier on, with the Champion Stakes as his ultimate objective.

17   *The Brigadier comes to his Waterloo*

The King George VI and the Queen Elizabeth Stakes took a little more out of the Brigadier than his previous efforts, since it was a day longer than after his other races before he regained his normal weight; but he never left an oat, pulled out as fresh and sound as usual and, so far as it was possible to discern, seemed to have suffered not the slightest ill effect from his exertions.

The Brigadier's next possible engagement was the Benson and Hedges Gold Cup at York in twenty-six days' time. It was a new, sponsored race, over one mile two furlongs and a hundred and ten yards, carrying a prize of nearly £40,000 to the winner.

It seemed an ideal target for the Brigadier, always provided the going was to his liking; and since we particularly wished northern racegoers to have the chance of seeing him and he was working as well as ever, we decided to send him to York.

It was a move which was made under auguries not entirely propitious. An old friend of mine, with great knowledge and experience of racing, who had been at Ascot, wrote to me that he hoped we would not run the Brigadier at York. He said that he thought he was tired when he came in after winning the King George VI and the Queen Elizabeth Stakes, but was too proud to show it, and that the race might have taken more out of him than was apparent. He added that the round course at York was a tricky one and over the years had produced more than a few false results and turn-ups.

Jean, too, had a feeling that she would rather he was not running and hoped that the weather might change, causing him to be withdrawn. One or two people told me after the race that, beforehand, they had a feeling that he was going to be beaten.

With the race three weeks ahead and the Brigadier thoroughly fit, it needed only normal work to keep him in trim; and when he left for York there was every indication that he was at his best.

Besides all this, the opposition did not seem particularly formidable.

Of his opponents, Roberto and Rheingold, who had fought out a desperate finish for the Derby – which went to the former by a short-head – were inseparable on form; but so ill suited was Rheingold to the Derby course that it seemed certain that anywhere other than Epsom the verdict would have gone his way. The class of the field in the Derby had given every impression of being below standard, for the time was slow and the third horse, Pentland Firth, was subsequently beaten three lengths in the Princess of Wales's Stakes at Newmarket by Falkland (Right Royal V–Argentina, by Nearco), who the previous year had failed by a neck and a head in a moderate St Leger, won by Athens Wood (Celtic Ash–Belle of Athens, by Acropolis) from Homeric.

The Derby winner Roberto (Hail to Reason–Bramalea, by Nashua) was bred in the United States by his owner, Mr J. W. Galbreath, and was trained in Ireland by Vincent O'Brien.

When Roberto was a two-year-old O'Brien, a highly competent and experienced trainer who has had many top-class horses through his hands and is therefore qualified to judge, was reported as saying that the colt was one of the best he had ever trained and that he considered him superior at that stage to Nijinsky and Sir Ivor, both outstanding horses and Derby winners.

After Roberto had won his first three races, a maiden event, the Anglesey Stakes and the National Stakes by, respectively, three lengths, six lengths and five lengths, it seemed that O'Brien's assessment might well be correct. Then came a sharp disappointment. Sent to Longchamp for the Grand Criterium, Roberto could only finish fourth to Hard to Beat, Steel Pulse and Prodice, beaten a neck, two lengths and two lengths.

I did not see any of Roberto's two-year-old races, but the consensus of informed opinion was that Lester Piggott, who has never found Longchamp the happiest of courses for him, left Roberto too much to do and that, in consequence, his running was not to be taken at face value.

Roberto's first race in 1972 was the Vauxhall Trial Stakes, seven furlongs, at Phoenix Park on 1 April. Ridden by Johnny Roe, who was Vincent O'Brien's stable jockey for all his runners in Ireland, Roberto won by a length and a half from Flair Path (Ragusa–Paddy's Flair, by Alcide), who had won his last race the previous year by four lengths; later in 1972 he finished third in the French Derby. The going was very heavy and of Roberto's performance *Raceform Notebook* remarks: 'he . . . went about his final business in workmanlike, if not brilliant, style and won well. In view of the very heavy going it is not easy to assess the value of the performance as a Guineas' trial.'

Roberto's next appearance was in the Two Thousand Guineas on 29 April. It was the first time that I had seen him and thus viewed him with interest. A tough-looking, workmanlike colt, with an honest head and largish ears, he had a deep body, well ribbed up, with good shoulders and powerful quarters, not the best of forelegs, but a good hind leg. The most striking impression he gave in general was that for a horse of his class he was markedly lacking in quality. Looking at him again after he had won the Derby, I observed to someone beside me: 'He looks the sort of horse you'd expect to see in the winner's enclosure after an Adjacent Hunts' race at a point-to-point.' He was not helped by his colour, being a dirty bay, and though he was a good hardy sort he certainly did not look the part of a classic horse.

Nevertheless in the Two Thousand, ridden by Bill Williamson, Roberto started second favourite at seven to two, leader in the market being High Top (Derring-Do–Camanae, by Vimy) with Willie Carson in the saddle and trained by Bernard van Cutsem for Sir Jules Thorn, a newcomer to racing who somewhat surprised Dick Hern standing beside him as the horses were at the post by asking: 'How far is this race?'

The official state of the going was good, but it had rained steadily since this verdict was pronounced and by the time the race was run the ground was on the soft side. The favourite High Top was a well-made, compact brown colt, typical of his sire Derring-Do, and had a commendable record behind him. He won three of his four races as a two-year-old, including the Observer Gold Cup, and prior to the Two Thousand was a winner by five lengths of the Yellow Pages Classic Trial at Thirsk. Going straight to the front, High Top kept up a strong gallop all the way and was still ahead at the winning post. Roberto seemed unable to match the speed of High Top out of the stalls, for he was trailing some half a dozen lengths behind him in the first four furlongs, but gradually made up the leeway until at the finish he was only half a length away from High Top and would have passed him with a bit farther to go. Five lengths behind Roberto, in third place, came the West Ilsley representative, Sun Prince.

It was a dour, honest performance on the part of Roberto, with no mark of brilliance about it, but indicated that the extra half mile in the Derby would probably be within his powers and that he must have an excellent chance of winning.

This Roberto succeeded in doing but, as related, on all available evidence the form of the race was poor by classic standards. The going was firm, which undoubtedly suited Roberto better than soft ground, and he had the advantage of all the power and skill of Lester Piggott, who was put up in place of Bill Williamson, in circumstances which drew the severest criticism of Roberto's owner and trainer from the public and the Press. The kindest observation that can be made on this distasteful episode is that Galbreath and O'Brien acted within the Rules of Racing and that, financially, Williamson was compensated adequately.

Though Roberto had had a really hard race in the Derby, he came out of it well – physically at least – and was confidently expected to follow in the footsteps of Nijinsky and add the Irish Sweeps Derby to his Epsom triumph.

Run on 1 July, the Irish classic came just over three weeks after the Derby. In accordance with his contract, Johnny Roe partnered Roberto, who was hot favourite at fifteen to eight. He was followed in the betting by the Irish Two Thousand Guineas winner Ballymore (3 to 1), the French colt Lyphard (7 to 2), Steel Pulse and Bog Road at 10 to 1 and Scottish Rifle (16 to 1). Backers were in for a shock. At no stage did Roberto ever hold a winning chance and finally trailed in twelfth of the fourteen runners. The winner was Steel Pulse, ridden by Bill Williamson, with Scottish Rifle second and Ballymore third.

Steel Pulse in the Derby at Epsom was not given much of a ride by Pyers and as a result finished eighth, behind Scottish Rifle who was sixth. At Ascot, Steel Pulse was five lengths behind Brigadier Gerard, receiving nineteen pounds – five pounds more than weight-for-age. This did not enhance the form in the Derby.

So bad was the running of Roberto that it could not be taken as true. The probability is that although he appeared none the worse physically, the desperately hard race which he had in the Derby when Piggott's flailing – though it did not hurt him because he was being slapped on the top of his rump where it is difficult to hit a horse hard – frightened the life out of him and, for the time being at any rate, deprived him of the zest for racing. That he was never in the hunt in the Irish Sweeps Derby probably turned out to be Roberto's salvation, since Roe appreciated that hitting him would be of no avail and, as a result, Roberto had an easy race, which helped to restore his confidence.

Until almost the last moment, Roberto was a doubtful runner for the Benson and Hedges Gold Cup. A few days before the race Lester Piggott went over to Ireland to ride Roberto a gallop in order to decide whether he would ride him or Rheingold at York, and Roberto went so badly that Lester at once plumped for Rheingold.

The mount on Roberto was then offered to Williamson, who had already accepted some rides for Mr David Robinson abroad. Vincent O'Brien telephoned John Galbreath to report the situation, whereupon Galbreath suggested that his American jockey, Braulio Baeza, a Panamanian, came over to ride Roberto, and this arrangement was made. Baeza had never ridden in England before, but held a deservedly high reputation in the United States and both Noel Murless and Sir Cecil Boyd-Rochfort, who had seen him in action, spoke very highly of him. Still, it was impossible to give Roberto a serious thought for the race. To start with, he seemed most unlikely to beat Barry Hill's candidate, Rheingold, who in his only race between Epsom and York had won the Grand Prix de Saint-Cloud by three lengths from Arlequino, with the French Derby winner, Hard to Beat, a further half length away third. This form flattered Rheingold, because Hard to Beat's trainer, Dick Carver, openly stated that the horse was not right and that he did not want to run him, the horse only being in the field at the owner's insistence. Moreover, Arlequino, in his previous race, had been beaten by the Queen's filly, Example, and subsequently Homeric gave him two pounds and beat him a neck; so that on these performances Rheingold could not be regarded as any great danger.

The Brigadier was accompanied to York by his half brother, Brigade Major, whom we sent up for two reasons: if the going changed suddenly and became soft, Brigade Major would run instead of the Brigadier, with a good chance of collecting some lucrative place money, and if he did not run, the journey without a race would benefit his volatile temperament. The faithful Almagest made up the party in his customary role.

Jean and I motored up to York on the Sunday night, staying at the Royal Station Hotel, in order to walk the course and watch the Brigadier canter on Tuesday morning.

We went to see the Brigadier after he had arrived at the racecourse stables on Monday afternoon. He was cool and composed, having travelled well. I thought that he had lost a little weight on the journey, but when I looked at him the next morning he appeared to have put it back.

It was a beautiful day when we arrived at the stables on Tuesday morning about 7 a.m., before the Brigadier and Almagest pulled out. Brigade Major was being led out by his lad, Vic Chitty, who used to look after his own brother, Town Major, so knew the peculiarities of the two inside-out.

Buster rode the Brigadier and Bob Asher was on Almagest; he did not do Almagest, but always rode him, as he was very light and the horse went well for him. Almagest did not have the best of mouths – he had cleared off one day on the way to the post and once with me up the canter at West Ilsley.

While we were watching the Brigadier and Almagest walking out, Roberto appeared, ridden by Baeza and led on a rein by the travelling lad. 'Even I don't have to go on a leading rein,' Jean remarked jokingly to the travelling lad, who laughed and replied, 'Oh, I'm not letting this one loose till ten past three this afternoon!'

I cannot say that Roberto impressed me any more than he did on Derby day.

The Knavesmire was a scene of activity; apart from the Brigadier, Almagest and Roberto, there were some local horses working there, and other visiting runners, including the Oaks winner Ginevra (Shantung–Zest, by Crepello), watched by her trainer, Ryan Price. In addition there was Brough Scott and his film team and the senior *Raceform* handicap expert, Tommy Watson.

The Brigadier looked magnificent, was full of himself and seemed in the best of form. We returned to the Station Hotel to breakfast, where the rival team of Galbreath, O'Brien and Baeza were also in the dining-room.

Having a drink in the bar to calm our nerves before leaving for the course, we encountered Sir Kenneth and Lady Butt, who had come to see Jacinth run in the Lowther Stakes, and joined them. We discussed our respective chances, agreeing that on known form both should win, a prognostication which proved sadly awry. Jacinth certainly preserved her unbeaten record, but elected to do so by refusing to enter the stalls.

A record crowd had gathered at York to see the Brigadier, for in no part of the country is a good and, especially, a fine-looking horse more appreciated than in Yorkshire; it was one of the reasons for our running the Brigadier at the meeting. It was almost impossible to move in the paddock and a crush of interested spectators surrounded the upper ring while the Brigadier was being saddled. During the proceedings the nose band broke. Buster immediately produced another one from his kit-bag and it was fitted in no time. Though a small incident, it was disturbing.

Watching the horses walking round the top ring before we saddled the Brigadier, I was standing with Sir Richard Sykes. As Roberto passed, Richard observed to me, 'It's difficult to believe we're looking at a Derby winner,' and I could not help but agree with him. As before the Derby, Roberto looked dry in his coat, though Noel Murless, Jack Waugh and George Blackwell, all good judges, thought that he carried more muscle than at Epsom.

On entering the main ring the Brigadier was greeted with a burst of applause, which he acknowledged by kicking up his heels. He looked with interest at the new surroundings and seemed as keen as ever to do battle.

Apart from Roberto and Rheingold, the field was made up with the indefatigable Gold Rod, ridden by Willie Carson, and Mill Reef's pace-maker, Bright Beam, with Geoff Lewis up. The going was very fast, suitable both to the Brigadier and Roberto.

As usual, we gave Joe an open brief, suggesting that as a general plan he should ride the Brigadier as he had done in the Prince of Wales Stakes at Ascot.

It was the first time that the Brigadier had raced on a left-handed course, but since all the gallops with a bend in them at West Ilsley are left handed, he was well accustomed to going round this way.

After seeing the Brigadier out of the ring, Dick and I walked through to the enclosure and just managed to squeeze into the owners' and trainers' stand, not having a particularly good view, but good enough for me to follow the course of the race by dint of a little neck stretching, not being so tall as Dick.

The betting went three to one on the Brigadier, seven to two Rheingold and twelve to one Roberto, an unprecedented price for a Derby winner in what was virtually a three-horse race, Gold Rod being at thirty-three to one and Bright Beam three hundred to one.

When the stalls opened, Baeza shot Roberto straight to the front. After a furlong, Bright Beam passed him and the pair opened up a clear lead, some six lengths ahead of Rheingold, the Brigadier being immediately behind the latter. They did not appear to be going an inordinately fast gallop, but it must have been a pretty good one as Bright Beam was done with when he ran wide coming round the final bend, where Baeza really set Roberto alight and again took up the running. Joe meanwhile had begun to move the Brigadier up past Rheingold and Bright Beam, going by them just after turning into the straight, where he was about three lengths behind Roberto. He had improved his position smoothly, and with the long straight ahead had plenty of time to tackle Roberto. The Brigadier got to Roberto's quarters, but when asked for a further effort could not gain on him.

Three furlongs out I knew he was beaten. Roberto showed no sign of stopping, though veering to the right towards the end of the race, which suggested that he had gone about as far as he liked at the terrific pace he had gathered. Wisely, Joe eased the Brigadier as soon as he realised that he had no chance of catching Roberto, so that the three lengths by which the

The Brigadier's only defeat, finishing second to Roberto in the Benson and Hedges Gold Cup,
York, 1972

Brigadier was beaten flatters Roberto.

There was no excuse: Roberto had galloped faster and reached the winning post first and that was all there was to it.

My first feeling was of bitter remorse – not at defeat, since defeat in itself is not the be all and end all of racing, but that I had let the Brigadier down by running him too soon after the King George VI and the Queen Elizabeth Stakes, which had taken the edge off him without my realising it. But the fantastically fast time, which stood up as reliable when compared with other times that day, and the fact that the video tape showed the Brigadier to have finished no less than seventeen lengths – the judge gave it as ten lengths – in front of Gold Rod, who ran on into third place after being last during the early stages, suggested that the Brigadier had run up to form.

Though saddened at the defeat of the Brigadier, the crowd gave both horses a great reception. The English public will always acclaim a good horse, whatever his nationality, and the coolness with which Roberto was received at Epsom was directed at his owner and trainer, not at the horse or the jockey.

Like his namesake, the Brigadier had at last come to his Waterloo, but like him, too, had borne himself gallantly.

Both Jean and I have been in racing too long to be unable to take defeat philosophically; those who cannot have no place on the Turf. After the race, she proposed that we went across to the racecourse stables to see the Brigadier, to assure him that we thought none the worse of him for not winning. We found him quite unmoved, indeed he had the air of a horse who had won, rather than of one who had just been beaten; as though he considered himself the moral victor if not the actual one.

The path to penury is paved with excuses for beaten horses, but when so momentous a turn-up occurs as in the Benson and Hedges Gold Cup, it is pertinent to examine every aspect concerning the chief actors in the drama, in this case Brigadier Gerard and Roberto.

Joe Mercer affirms that, as the race was run, there was no excuse. In some quarters he has been criticised for giving the Brigadier too much to do, in which respect it is interesting to refer back to the shattering defeat of Fairway by Royal Minstrel in the Eclipse Stakes of 1929, when Tommy Weston on Fairway was criticised for laying up too near his pacemaker Bosworth! Had any of us realised that Roberto was going to put up the performance he did, and that Rheingold would prove a broken reed, we would have agreed upon tactics of ignoring every horse in the race bar Roberto and sitting on his tail; even so, I doubt whether the result would have been different and Joe thinks the same.

One can sometimes misjudge a horse through being too close to him; and while the Brigadier seemed to us all as well as ever, Geoff Lewis remarked to Ian Balding in the parade ring: 'The Brigadier doesn't seem himself to me; he looks worried. You'll see, he'll get beaten today.' And Lester Piggott, a shrewd judge not given to lightly considered statements, told me that in his view the race for the King George VI and the Queen Elizabeth Stakes had taken the edge off him for the time being.

Regarding the Brigadier himself, one important point emerged: when he got back to the stables at York after the race, and put his head down, a large clot of mucus came out of one of his nostrils. This could well have impaired his breathing perceptibly and, in a race of this tempo, made the difference between winning and losing.

The Brigadier was not favoured by the weight-for age scale, which at that time required him to give Roberto eleven pounds. Under the new scale he would only be giving him nine pounds. Thus, owing to a combination of factors, it seems probable that the Brigadier ran a little below his top form, a conclusion arrived at by Timeform's *Racehorses of 1972*, in which is expressed the carefully considered, rational and reliable opinion of a team of experts.

The mystery of the Benson and Hedges Gold Cup is: how did Roberto come to produce at least a stone of improvement on any of his previous or subsequent efforts?

To start with, Roberto undoubtedly is at his best on firm going. Like the Brigadier, he has won in every type of ground, but it is firm ground that he really likes.

Secondly, against top-class horses he is a one-pacer. Sent along from start to finish, he is a formidable opponent, but held up for a late run he cannot quicken sufficiently to cope with good horses. He showed this in the Grand Criterium and the Two Thousand Guineas. The ten-furlong course at York, with the first six on the turn, is an ideal front-runners' course.

Thirdly, though he won the Derby it seems possible that Roberto's best distance is short of one and a half miles. It was, perhaps, a combination of Piggott's strong riding, Roberto's own courage and the moderate calibre of the opposition, rather than true stamina, that got him first past the winning post in the Derby.

But even all these factors operating together do not seem to account for his record-breaking performance.

Following his victory at York, Roberto was sent over for the Prix Niel, one mile and three furlongs, at Longchamp on 10 September, presumably to give him experience of the course before he contested the Prix de l'Arc de Triomphe. He was opposed by Hard to Beat, Toujours Pret and Vitaner. The going was yielding and Baeza flew over from America to ride him. Jean and I went to see the race.

Roberto ran tamely; he simply was not the same horse that we had seen at York. Hard to Beat set off in front with Roberto following close behind, apparently taking no more than just a nice hold of his bit. At no stage did Roberto ever look like overhauling Hard to Beat, on whom Lester Piggott won by a somewhat comfortable length. It was an uninspiring performance on the part of Roberto, even allowing for the going being softer than he liked, and difficult to reconcile with the dash he showed at York and with his commendable effort in heavy going when he won in Ireland at the start of the season.

I had hoped that Roberto's connections might have been tempted to have another cut at the Brigadier, in the Champion Stakes, since a mile and a quarter had seemed to suit Roberto so well. On account of the weight-for-age scale changing with the advance of the year, the weights in the Champion Stakes favoured the Brigadier by four pounds as compared with York and almost certainly the race would have been run to suit him better than the Benson and Hedges Gold Cup, because the relentless straight at Newmarket does not enable front-running tactics to be exploited as effectively as at York. It is difficult to believe that had there been any confidence in Roberto's ability to beat Brigadier Gerard in the Champion Stakes he would not have met this engagement, since victory in the race would have made John Galbreath both leading owner and breeder for 1972 and Vincent O'Brien leading trainer, honours which no man forgoes lightly. Roberto dodged the Champion Stakes in favour of the Arc de Triomphe, in which he had everything to gain and little to lose.

When the Arc de Triomphe came round, on 8 October, the ground had dried up and the going was good, appreciably firmer than in the Prix Niel. We went over for the race and watched Roberto with especial interest.

Roberto seemed a good deal more on his toes in the paddock than before the previous race at Longchamp, and in the hot autumn afternoon was sweating. Though well muscled up, he looked a little rough and dull in his coat, but eager to gallop. This last impression was soon borne out, for he went down to the post as if jet-propelled and when the stalls opened shot out as he had done at York, an entirely different horse from the almost disinterested animal we had seen in the Prix Niel. Before covering a furlong Roberto was several lengths in front, galloping as if he was haunted. So he continued, informed spectators wondering whether Baeza had taken leave of his senses. For it is common knowledge that at Longchamp, as at Epsom, to burst a horse up the hill in the first five furlongs of the mile-and-a-half course is suicide to the chance of winning, especially in so strongly contested a race as the Arc de Triomphe. Thus Roberto continued at a pace which guaranteed that long before he reached the winning post he would be a spent force. And so it proved. Though he was still in front at ten furlongs and trying hard to hang on, his chance of winning had gone. Eventually he finished seventh, six lengths behind the winner San San (Bald Eagle–Sail Navy), a filly bred in the U.S.A. and ridden by Freddie Head in the colours of Countess Margit Batthyany. Hard to Beat finished eighth, a length and a half behind Roberto.

It seemed inconceivable that so intelligent a jockey and good judge of pace as Baeza should ride Roberto into the ground in this manner, for choice; so that it was not surprising to learn afterwards that Baeza stated that his tactics were not his own, but were dictated by his being unable to hold Roberto.

So ended the season for this Jekyll and Hyde horse, whose performances left several questions to be answered.

How did he come to produce form in the Benson and Hedges Gold Cup at least a stone superior to that shown in any of his previous or subsequent races? Why was it that, after his tame performance in the Prix Niel, he should gallop in the Prix de l'Arc de Triomphe as if possessed by the devil? What is his true measure as a racehorse and what is his best distance?

Roberto's four-year-old career up to the time of writing, 6 September, has been one of withdrawal, bloodless victory and ignominious defeat.

He was withdrawn from the Prix Ganay, having hit himself on the morning of the race. On his first appearance of the season, in the Nijinsky Stakes, ten furlongs, at Leopardstown, he was beaten three-quarters of a length by Ballymore at level weights.

In the Coronation Cup he beat Attica Meli, who had lost her form. Though his time, 2 minutes, 34.49 seconds, was within 0.69 seconds of Mahmoud's record, this was beaten the next day by Knockroe, a five-year-old gelding who carried 6 lb more. These times were undoubtedly due to the exceptionally fast ground.

Roberto did not contest the Eclipse Stakes, on the excuse that the going was too soft and in one place false. The connections of the other runners in the Eclipse were not deterred from starting their horses.

In the King George VI and the Queen Elizabeth Stakes he faded right out of the picture to finish last but one, beating only Park Lawn, pace-maker for Weaver's Hall, and he was withdrawn from the Benson and Hedges Gold Cup on the morning of the race.

In the light of hindsight we should have given the Brigadier a longer rest after the King George VI and the Queen Elizabeth Stakes, instead of taking him to York. The race looked cut and dried for him on form and no one could have foretold that it would have taken a record-beating performance to win it; but at this level of competition the one chance which it is dangerous to take is that of not giving a horse enough time to return to his absolute best after a hard race. He may look, eat and work well, be his correct weight and show no outward sign that he is not as good as ever; but only the racecourse test will supply the true answer, and if the horse has been brought out again too soon the penalty may have to be paid. In perhaps ninety-nine cases out of a hundred we would have got away with it, but in this instance the hundredth case was Roberto producing so phenomenal an improvement out of the hat. But if a horse has once shown real brilliance, whether at home or on the racecourse, there is always the chance that some day, somewhere he will reproduce it. There is no doubt that, fundamentally, Roberto was a good horse when the Jekyll in him superseded the Hyde.

Nevertheless, he cannot be classed as more than good on his day, for he was too erratic and one of the first requirements of a top-class racehorse is consistency.

18 *A Record-breaking Comeback*

While no one likes to see his horse beaten, leastwise when previously he has always passed the winning post first, defeat can be a valuable factor in assessing the qualities of a racehorse, because it reveals both his mental and physical resilience – or lack of it. Often, horses who have been beaten after a successful run of victories never win again; either the physical exertion of the fatal race leaves an indelible mark, or his morale crumbles; and when next he is called upon to do battle he caves in. So it was of the utmost importance for the Brigadier to race again before he retired, in order to give him the chance to re-establish his reputation and prove that his defeat had left him unimpaired in mind and body.

He was engaged in the Queen Elizabeth II Stakes, but we had not intended to run him in this race as he had won it the previous year and it had been earmarked for the Brigadier's stable companion Sun Prince.

Apart from the Champion Stakes, the other race in which the Brigadier was entered was the Cumberland Lodge Stakes at Ascot, the distance of which had been changed by the Ascot authority from a mile and a half to ten furlongs, presumably in the hope of bringing about a meeting between the Brigadier and Mill Reef before the former contested the Champion Stakes and the latter the Arc de Triomphe, for Mill Reef was back in good work and as yet had not met with his tragic accident.

Then Sun Prince had a setback in the shape of a fractured splint bone, not a serious injury but one which finished his racing for the season. This left the Queen Elizabeth II Stakes open to the Brigadier, if we chose, and we decided to go for this race instead of the Cumberland Lodge Stakes, as it carried more prestige.

Though the Brigadier lost 22 lb on the round trip to York, this was not an inordinate amount in view of the distance travelled and he soon put it back again. In fact, despite having been really stretched by Roberto he did not have so hard a race as in the King George VI and Queen Elizabeth Stakes, since he was eased some way from home.

The Queen Elizabeth II Stakes was due to be run on 23 September, which gave him exactly seven weeks from the day of his York race. It was ample time to enable him to recover completely from his previous effort and be brought to the peak of fitness by the day. He behaved and progressed with that exemplary consistency which we all had come to regard as part of him. As I had ventured to predict, he seemed to have improved since York and to be moving better than ever. He was kept mostly to six-furlong and seven-furlong work, and to give him a change of scenery before he went to Ascot we arranged for him to gallop at Newbury after racing on Saturday, 16 September, exactly a week before the Ascot race. We announced this to the Press, so that any racegoers who wished to do so could stay to see him work. It was no more than an exercise gallop over seven furlongs in company with Almagest, the only difference being that it was staged at Newbury instead of on the West Ilsley downs.

There was a good attendance on the day, a number of people having come to Newbury especially to see the Brigadier in action. He always liked playing to the gallery and seemed pleased to have an audience, his previous gallop at Newbury having been conducted in private. He did not disappoint his admirers. Ridden by Joe, he strode past Almagest in the last furlong of the seven-furlong spin, passing the post with his ears pricked to a round of applause which he thoroughly appreciated. Though the rust of autumn had begun to tinge his coat he looked magnificent, full of muscle, heavier than before and the very picture of well-being, a real tribute to Dick and his stable staff.

We were confident that at Ascot he would prove himself not merely back to form but better than ever.

We wanted the Brigadier to come back with éclat and resolved that there could be no more effective way of his doing so than by breaking the record for Ascot's Old Mile, which had stood for fifteen years. Having established the intention we considered the method, deciding that Almagest, ridden by Jimmy Lindley, should be put in to set a really hot gallop for as long as he lasted, which should be to about the turn into the straight, and that Joe and the Brigadier should then take over and make the best of their way home, not letting up till they were past the winning post.

Conditions favoured our purpose: the weather was warm and fine, the going firm and it seemed that the good fortune which, except in the St James's Palace Stakes, had always favoured us at Ascot was about to smile on us again.

Only two horses opposed the Brigadier, apart from Almagest. These were our old rival Sparkler, ridden by Lester Piggott, to whom the Brigadier was set to give seven pounds, and Redundant, a three-year-old trained by Noel Murless, ridden by Geoff Lewis and a winner last time out of a thousand-pound mile handicap carrying 9 st 10 lb, of another similar race and the Britannia Stakes at Royal Ascot.

Almagest was drawn No. 1, on the outside, then Redundant, Sparkler and, on the rails, the Brigadier.

When the stalls opened, to my horror, all the runners emerged except Brigadier Gerard, who followed them some three lengths behind. It transpired that he had been sitting back on the rear door of the stalls, and though Joe had shouted to the starter not to let them go the official had disregarded this plea and pressed the button. My first reaction was: 'There goes our hope of breaking the record.' Jimmy Lindley, as arranged, had gone to the front on Almagest and after a couple of furlongs was looking back anxiously, wondering what had happened to the Brigadier.

Redundant followed Almagest, then came Sparkler, with the Brigadier in on the rails in last place, but right on Sparkler's heels. I was not worried by the Brigadier's position, only sorry that the chance of his breaking the record seemed to have vanished. Almagest had run out of steam and

The Brigadier tracking Redundant and Sparkler before going on to win the Queen Elizabeth II Stakes, Ascot, 1972

Finish of the King George VI and the Queen Elizabeth Stakes, won from Parnell and Riverman (obscurred by the Brigadier)

dropped back four furlongs from home, Redundant turning into the straight pressed by Sparkler, with the Brigadier hard on Sparkler's heels, still on the fence. Joe would have to pull out and come round the leading pair, as there was no chance of his getting through on the rails. Sparkler took over from Redundant soon after the two had squared up for home and at the distance Joe brought the Brigadier out, preparatory to launching his final attack.

As usual, the Brigadier took about three strides to reach his full momentum. As he attained it, he was coming into the last furlong and from there he left Sparkler standing, opening up an ever-increasing gap till, at the post, he was six lengths clear. It was a staggering performance, the seal being set on it when the discovery was made that he had beaten the record by over a second, and he received a deserved ovation. The Brigadier had re-established himself with a vengeance, running one of the finest races of his career.

It was especially pleasing in that it showed the resilience of his physical powers and morale, both of which had proved untouched by defeat, reflecting the words of his namesake in one of the most desperate situations of his *Adventures* and *Exploits*: 'I have a spirit like a slip of steel, for the more you bend it the higher it springs.'

Before the Champion Stakes was due to be run, twenty-four shares in the Brigadier had been sold to private breeders, the terms giving Jean and myself complete powers over the direction of his future, so that he could never be sold abroad.

Though the decision also rested with us as to whether he met his engagement in the Champion Stakes, or not, we felt that we should establish that at least a majority of the shareholders should be agreeable to his doing so.

Every single shareholder consulted wanted him to run, a most encouraging attitude for this day and age, when many in their position would have preferred the safer path of allowing him to rest on his regained and glorious laurels, to risking a final and irrevocable defeat, with its consequent loss to his prestige and value. All of us concerned in the Brigadier were delighted.

Despite the downfall in the Champion Stakes of past heroes such as Colorado, Ballymoss, Royal Palace and Nijinsky, we were confident that a similar fate would not overcome the Brigadier. He was at the height of his powers, had no chinks in his armour apart from heavy going, in which case he would not be started, and on form had the beating of all his probable opponents. He could only be defeated by an act of fate, which is an integral hazard of racing and must be faced.

So, the die was cast and the Champion Stakes became the Brigadier's final exploit. This race came exactly three weeks after the Queen Elizabeth Stakes, on Saturday, 14 October.

As before the Ascot race, Dick thought that the Brigadier would benefit from having his final gallop on Newbury racecourse, as opposed to completing his whole preparation at home.

When the morning of the Brigadier's gallop at Newbury dawned there was a fairly dense fog; so much so, that I wondered whether we should be able to work the horses at all. However, it cleared just sufficiently for the purpose, though it would have been too foggy to race.

The Brigadier and Almagest were going seven furlongs the reverse way of the course, that is to say right handed, finishing at the Greenham end of the back straight. The going was beautiful, a real credit to Frank Osgood, who always has the Newbury course in such good order. While the Brigadier knew exactly where he was, he had always galloped and raced up the straight, as the races are run, so was interested to find himself undergoing a different routine. He also realised that he was working towards his horse box and was alert and eager.

Fog sometimes has a disturbing effect on horses, perhaps because they can lose their sense of direction in it, causing them to want to go faster, possibly in the hope of getting out of the fog as soon as possible; and I remember the now-successful trainer 'Fiddler' Goodwill, when he was working for the late Tom Leader, making about six circuits of the Links at Newmarket after the rest of us in the gallop had pulled up, before he succeeded in stopping the mare he was riding.

Happily no such misadventure befell the Brigadier, but he certainly worked with great zest.

There was a dramatic quality about the scene as we stood peering through the Cimmerian gauze, waiting for the horses to emerge. Nothing could be seen of the stands across the course, the silence was complete; we might have been in outer space. Then, faintly at first and gradually increasing, came that unmistakable and thrilling sound, which in two thousand years no writer has succeeded in describing better than Virgil with his, 'quadripedante putrem sonitu quatit ungula campum' – the hoofbeats of galloping horses – and out of the fog burst the Brigadier as he swept past Almagest. At a few yards' distance from him at which I was standing as he passed, he was a magnificent and awe-inspiring sight, ears pricked, nostrils distended, his great, powerful frame and limbs moving with the rhythm and force of an express train, his hooves tearing the turf from under him – my heart bled for Frank's groundsmen – the momentum of his progress leaving the swishing of its slip-stream behind him. His sense of direction beamed on the end of the back straight, where his horse box awaited him, and determined to get there as fast as possible, he was really travelling. In a flash he had vanished into the fog, his hooves beating out in diminuendo until, once again, there was silence.

Never had I seen him work more impressively and in this form I was convinced that no horse in the world was capable of beating him.

With a good heart we faced the Brigadier's last battle, his second Champion Stakes. It was just a matter of all keeping well with him and the weather being kind to us. In both respects fortune favoured us: the Brigadier remained in perfect order and the fine weather held.

19   *The Brigadier's Last Battle*

As usual, I stayed with Jim Joel at Sefton Lodge for the Newmarket meeting. The Champion Stakes was run on the Saturday, the same day as the Cesarewitch, for which Jim had the favourite, The Admiral (Salvo–Isola d'Asti, by Court Harwell), a tall bay three-year-old colt, who had won three races and been placed second three times from eight starts that season. Trained by Noel Murless and ridden by Tony Murray, The Admiral looked to have a favourite's chance, so there was every hope that the two chief races of the day would fall to the party at Sefton Lodge.

After the disastrous manner in which the weather had turned against us the previous year, it was with some anxiety that I viewed the morning when I left the house early on Saturday to go to the racecourse stables. Greatly to my relief, it was dry. Jim's chauffeur, Neville, drove me and it was still dark when we arrived. At seven o'clock in the morning the traffic in Newmarket High Street is rather lighter than it is later in the day, so we got to the stable some fifteen minutes before the horses were ready to pull out.

As I sat waiting for the time to pass, I thought with a little sadness that this was the last occasion the Brigadier would ever do a canter on the morning of a race. His term of duty in this sphere was almost over, his final exploit on the Turf lay only a few hours ahead. If he was beaten, he would never have the opportunity of retrieving such misfortune with a victory; he would end his racing career, as have many great horses before him, with a defeat. Nothing could deprive him of his great record, but there is all the difference in the world between going out on top and failing the last test. However brilliant a horse may have been, once his sparkle has gone, never to be rekindled, a speck of tarnish is left on his reputation which cannot be erased. But if a great horse can finish with a worthy victory, the stigma of a past defeat is forgiven; it is the final battle that really counts.

Thus, despite his outstanding achievements, the Brigadier's last race meant much to his place in posterity. It would be a sad day for him if he was beaten. But that he would win, I felt sure. Apart from his superb condition and morale, the real test had come in the Queen Elizabeth II Stakes, his first race after his single downfall. Had he failed then, the writing would have been on the wall: he was past his best. Instead he had put up, perhaps, the greatest performance of his career, showing that, far from having gone over the top, he had moved from strength to strength.

Soon Dick arrived and the Brigadier and Almagest came out of the yard. After walking round for a little, they hack cantered down between the Links and the main road, crossed to the racecourse side of the Heath and walked towards the Cambridgeshire start, preparatory to cantering back between the Ditches. We drove down to see them across the road and, some way off, caught sight of two figures and a horse. They proved to be Alec Head and Comte Roland de Chambure, the horse being Alec's charge and our chief rival, Riverman, who had also come out to do a canter.

Dick and I climbed the bank of the Ditch nearest the Rowley Mile course and down the other side, to await the Brigadier and Almagest as they cantered by. We noted how much better the going was on the West Ilsley gallops than between the Ditches, which was not surprising in view of the far greater number of horses trained at Newmarket. Soon Almagest came by, followed by the Brigadier, crackling his nostrils as he sometimes liked to do; I have heard it said that this is the sign of a stayer, but have no proof of it. The Brigadier moved in easy, relaxed style, ridden as customary in the circumstances by Buster.

When he had passed, we climbed to the top of the Ditch on our way back to the car. As we came over the rise, Riverman was cantering by on the other side. Our sudden appearance startled him and he ducked to one side, understandably causing his rider to express his displeasure in no uncertain terms. Unwittingly we might have sabotaged the chance of our most dangerous opponent had Riverman shed his pilot and got loose, but fortunately all was well and he cantered on, his composure regained.

We apologised to Alec, who replied: 'If anything had happened to Riverman you'd have had to give me a share in Brigadier Gerard to make up for it!'

After seeing the Brigadier back to the stable, I returned to Sefton Lodge for breakfast and to await the race. As opposed to the same period before the Two Thousand and the Champion Stakes the previous year, I felt confident and at ease, almost as if the Brigadier had already won, so strong was the sense of impending victory.

Early on, the morning, though dry, had been dull and grey, but now the sun came out and the day blossomed into one of warmth and autumnal beauty, such as Newmarket in its softer moods can produce. It seemed a good omen and a fair swing back of the pendulum in favour of the Brigadier, after his ordeal by rain and mud in his previous Champion Stakes.

Jean arrived for lunch and, fortified by its excellence, we left early for the course.

The last appearance of the Brigadier, the running of the Cesarewitch, always a favourite race with the public, and the mellowness of the day blended to draw an extra large crowd, so that it was as well that we had started in good time.

A full programme lay ahead, since the division of the Snailwell Maiden race for two-year-olds brought the number of races up to eight. The Cesarewitch was third on the card, the Champion Stakes fifth.

The opening event, the first division of the Snailwell Maiden Stakes, went to Mystic Circle (Aureole–My Enigma, by Klairon), a nice filly owned and bred by my friend and partner in Turf Newspapers, Tom Blackwell, for whom she was trained by Bruce Hobbs. I had a certain interest in Mystic Circle, having persuaded Tom to buy her grandam, Land of Hope, at the December Sales. Bred by the late Cecily Lambton, Land of Hope (by Court Martial) traces eventually to the Oaks winner, Canterbury Pilgrim, dam of Swynford and Chaucer.

. This victory of one friend would, I hoped, be the prelude to that of another, Jim Joel, with The Admiral in the Cesarewitch. When The Admiral struck the front, apparently with a double handful and the race well won, it certainly looked as if this was to be; but he weakened quickly inside the last furlong and was run out of it by Cider with Rosie (Ballyciptic–Devon Brew, by Whiteway), a tough, game four-year-old filly trained by Staff Ingham and ridden by Taffy Thomas.

Still backward and immature, The Admiral probably weakened because he had not yet reached his full strength, rather than through lack of stamina.

With an apprentices' race intervening, many racegoers took the opportunity to get a look at the runners for the Champion Stakes, rather than watch the event in progress.

Eight opposed the Brigadier: his former opponents Riverman (Freddie Head), Steel Pulse (Bill Williamson) and Lord David (Geoff Lewis), Sol Argent (Frankie Durr), winner of his previous race, a handicap at Lingfield, under 9 st 7 lb, Boreen (Buster Parnell), an Irish colt who had beaten

Pistol Packer at Deauville last time out, Jimsun (Jimmy Lindley), a three-year-old who had run fourth in the Cambridgeshire carrying 8 st 12 lb, L'Apache (Eric Eldin), a useful horse in 1971, who had lost his form, and the Brigadier's stable companion Almagest (Tony Murray).

We put in Almagest to ensure that the Brigadier should not have to make his own running, tactics which would have been undesirable for the Brigadier over a mile and a quarter across the flat. By now the Brigadier had developed into an exceptionally powerful horse, took a strong hold and, with nothing but ten furlongs straight expanse of the Rowley Mile course between him and the winning post, he might have run too freely had he been forced to go to the front from the start.

As ever, the Brigadier outshone his rivals in the paddock and looked trained to perfection – no mean feat on the part of Dick, for he had been racing fit since early in the season, had met every engagement planned for him, had always run up to form and was still at the peak of condition.

The late afternoon sun played on his coat which, though its summer sheen was dimmed by the rime of autumn, held that warm glow which betokens a horse in really good order. Heavier than at any time before, he was the embodiment of power blended with the easy grace of a panther. Even against handsome horses such as Riverman and Lord David, the pick of the opposition in the paddock, he looked unbeatable.

As Dick, Joe, Buster and I stood together in the parade ring, with Almagest's rider Tony Murray the odd-man-out, a sense of finality hung over us. For three years we had been assembling thus before the Brigadier's races and this was the last time we would do so. Together we had experienced all the anxieties and stresses that go with that brief span before the horses leave the paddock; and there had been times when, on account of the possible outcome, the tension had been momentous. In some ways it was a relief to think that in a few moments these ordeals, so far as the Brigadier was concerned, would be over for good. At the same time we would miss them, for they had formed a bond of comradeship between us, which would leave a memory never to be eroded.

Among the crowd assembled round the perimeter of the ring, one felt that a like feeling pervaded; the murmur of conversation and comment that drifted across towards us was strangely subdued, almost as if coming from a congregation in church before the service began. Virtually everyone among them was hoping to see the Brigadier win and to be spared the sadness of seeing a champion fail in his last race.

We had arranged for Tony Murray to go on with Almagest, so that Joe would be certain of a lead for at least seven furlongs, should no other runner wish to make running. Apart from that, Joe would ride the race as it came up.

Soon the preliminaries were over and the horses were going down to the start, Almagest fighting for his head and giving Tony a far from pleasant ride, the Brigadier lobbing down casually, conserving his energy for the return journey.

A slight haze hung over the Heath and in the pale sunshine the visibility was as if one was looking through a veil of gossamer: horses, grass and jockeys' silks all had a softness of colouring, of which a clearer atmosphere would have deprived them.

Dick and I went up to our usual place on the roof of the stand to watch the race. Despite the haze, it was not difficult to pick out the runners in the small field.

According to plan, Almagest went off in front, followed by L'Apache and Steel Pulse, with the Brigadier, Lord David and Boreen most prominent of the others. Steel Pulse took over from Almagest after four furlongs, though Almagest stuck to him for another furlong or so.

Four furlongs out it was clear that the Brigadier would win. He was tucked in behind Steel Pulse and going so strongly that Joe had no easy task in restraining him. Three furlongs from home he was forced to ease the Brigadier out from behind Steel Pulse, for fear of striking into his heels. As soon as he saw daylight the Brigadier took command and set off for the winning post, fully a furlong before Joe wanted to make his effort. As he opened up a clear lead, the crowd began to cheer him home as they had done so often in the past, this time more enthusiastically than ever, for it was the last chance they would have of doing so. Meanwhile Riverman, on whom Freddie Head had ridden a well-judged waiting race, struggled nobly to catch the Brigadier and, as the latter eased up slightly having been in front so long, Riverman got to within a length and a half of him, but long before the winning post the result was assured.

Thus ended the Brigadier's final exploit, in a victory achieved with all the self-confidence and insouciance of his namesake, beating the best horse up to ten furlongs in France, in a race worthy of the occasion and on a course offering the truest and most searching test of a racehorse in the world.

He had barely passed the post when the crowd began running to see him come in; and as he walked proudly back through the passage made by his admirers he was given a reception worthy of his greatness.

Joe slipped off the Brigadier's back, unsaddled, gave him a final pat and paused to stand by his head at the behest of the photographers. Even in this

The Brigadier returning to the winner's enclosure after his last race, the Champion Stakes,
Newmarket, 1972

triumphant moment I thought he looked sad: it was the end of an epic partnership and he felt it deeply.

As he stood in the winner's enclosure, someone called for three cheers for the Brigadier and they sounded out across the Heath, a tribute I have never heard given at Newmarket in forty years. The scene was very moving, touching the heart of every lover of a great, gallant horse and of the best traditions of English racing. The 'take the horses away' came to signify that all was well, and the Brigadier left the unsaddling enclosure to a final round of applause, walking across the paddock and off the racecourse for good.

20 Postscript

The Brigadier returned to West Ilsley from Newmarket to be let down and roughed off, preparatory to going to his new home at the Egerton Stud, where he was born.

I was very happy that he was able to stand at the Egerton Stud, as I have known Lady Macdonald-Buchanan, who owns the stud, and Sir Reginald, her husband, from my days at Clarehaven and Michel Grove, also Jack Waugh the present manager, who was assistant trainer to Basil Jarvis when I first went to Newmarket; and it was through me that the present stud groom, Cornish, went to Egerton. I had advertised for a man to work on my own stud and Cornish, who had previously been with point-to-point horses, applied for the post. When I interviewed him, I realised that his potential was far above that which the job with me could offer, explained this to him and suggested that I tried to find him a place at a top-class stud, where he would have greater scope for advancement. I spoke about him to Michael Oswald, who was then stud manager at Egerton and now occupies this position to the Queen, the outcome being that Cornish was taken on and under the tuition of that outstanding stud groom, Podmore, who has now retired, worked his way up to his present position.

I do not know of a pleasanter or better-managed stud than Egerton, and there is nowhere that I would prefer the Brigadier to spend the rest of his days than there.

When the Brigadier was ready to leave West Ilsley, Jean and I journeyed to Egerton to see him in. Buster, Williamson and Peter West, the horse-box driver, travelled with him.

He arrived on a pleasant, mellow afternoon, to be received by Jack Waugh, Cornish, his future stallion-man Wally Hunt and ourselves, Podmore doing him the honour of coming over from his home to see him in, having been present at the Brigadier's birth, before his retirement.

The Brigadier stepped proudly and gently from his box and walked quietly to his new quarters, was introduced to Wally Hunt and then expressed interest in the contents of his manger.

When he was loosed in his paddock for the first time, he looked at us as if he was viewing exhibits at the zoo, turning away and starting to graze. Only when we left him did he show any sign of perturbation, perhaps through lack of company, as he started to neigh and gallop round the paddock. After two or three circuits each way, he pulled up and settled down once more to grazing.

He made the acquaintance of Royal Palace, with whom he sometimes takes his morning exercise, preferring to go in front, to which Royal Palace proved agreeable. As at West Ilsley, his behaviour has never been anything but admirable and he has been quick to learn and perfect all that is required of him. He has filled out and let down, but like his sire, Queen's Hussar, and his ancestor Fairway, thrice present in his pedigree, he does not give the impression that he will ever become gross. We visit him frequently and he is always pleased to see us.

When the Brigadier had proved his brilliance on the racecourse, we determined to have him portrayed at the peak of racing condition as a four-year-old.

For this task Jean and I agreed that there was only one person in the world we wanted, the sculptor, Professor J. R. Skeaping, R.A., whose technical knowledge of horses and genius in portraying them places him head and shoulders above any living artist in this sphere, whether painter or sculptor. John Skeaping is an old friend of mine, whom I first met when we were serving together in the S.A.S. towards the end of World War II. A Rome Prize winner, his many notable works include the superb, life-size statues in bronze of Hyperion and Chamossaire at Newmarket. We decided that only thus could the Brigadier be portrayed in a manner worthy of him, that we would approach John Skeaping with a view to his undertaking the commission and that he alone of artists would see the Brigadier for the purpose of depicting him.

John agreed to the proposal and thus his sculpture is the sole official portrait of the Brigadier and the only one for which he has posed.

A keen follower of racing, a former hunting man and amateur rider with an expert knowledge of equine anatomy, John knew the Brigadier well, had seen him race and admired him greatly, pronouncing him the best-looking and most perfectly formed horse he had ever seen in his life. During the summer of 1972 John started to work on the project. He saw the Brigadier frequently, took the fullest and most detailed measurements of him, during which the Brigadier stood like a rock, and innumerable photographs.

Professor John Skeaping R.A. working on the model of his life-size statue of the Brigadier

The Brigadier leads Royal Palace at exercise at the Egerton Stud, Newmarket

From the beginning the clay model went well and it was clear that John had captured every physical detail of the Brigadier and also his character. In consequence, the statue progressed with remarkable speed and fluency. Jean and I made several visits to John's studio at Castries, near the Camargue, to see how the work was developing and so that we could check every detail; and John journeyed to England whenever he wanted to study a particular feature of the Brigadier and compare him in his mind with the model. He could describe every detail of the horse's conformation out of his head.

By coincidence, the clay model was ready for casting just as I was finishing the manuscript of this book. When completed in bronze, the statue will stand in the grounds of East Woodhay House and if in the course of time no home can be found for it in the family, it will pass to the Jockey Club.

The Brigadier's first runners will appear in 1976 and if they possess even part of those qualities which made him one of the greatest racehorses and certainly the best miler bred in Europe this century, he will do much to maintain the English thoroughbred in that position of supremacy which has made him the envy of all nations from the time of his evolution.

Appendices

NEWBURY, *24 June 1970*

Berkshire Stakes, £1,201, 5 furlongs straight, two-year-old colts and fillies.

1	Brigadier Gerard, 8 st 5 lb	J. Mercer
2	Mais'y Dotes, 8 st 7 lb	P. Tulk
3	Porter's Precinct (U.S.A.), 8 st 6 lb	D. Keith
4	Young and Foolish, 8 st 10 lb	L. Piggott
5	Irish Conquest, 8 st 10 lb	B. Taylor

Won by 5 lengths, 2½ lengths.
8/15 Young and Foolish, 4/1 Mais'y Dotes, 9/1 Porter's Precinct, 100/7 Brigadier Gerard and Irish Conquest.

Time: 1 m 6 s

SALISBURY, *2 July 1970*

Champagne Stakes, £598 2s., 6 furlongs straight, two-year-old colts and fillies.

1	Brigadier Gerard, 9 st 7 lb	J. Mercer
2	Gaston Again, 9 st 0 lb	G. Lewis
3	Comedy Star (U.S.A.), 8 st 12 lb	G. Ramshaw
4	Amberwin, 8 st 12 lb	J. Lindley
5	Uncle Sol, 8 st 12 lb	A. Barclay
6	Captain Teach, 8 st 12 lb	R. P. Elliott
7	Pink Shantung, 8 st 9 lb	E. Hide
8	Russian Reward, 8 st 5 lb	R. Marshall
9	Director, 8 st 12 lb	W. Williamson
10	Sandy Lane, 8 st 12 lb	P. Cook

Won by 4 lengths, neck.
8/13 Brigadier Gerard, 4/1 Gaston Again, 7/1 Uncle Sol, 100/8 Comedy Star, 100/7 Director, 25/1 others.

Time: not taken

NEWBURY, 15 August 1970

Washington Singer Stakes, £1,154 16s., 6 furlongs straight, two-year-old colts and geldings.

1	Brigadier Gerard, 9 st 2 lb	J. Mercer
2	Comedy Star (U.S.A.), 8 st 10 lb	J. Lindley
3	Takasaki, 8 st 10 lb	A. Murray
4	Hello, 8 st 10 lb	R. Hutchinson
5	Hill Command (U.S.A.), 8 st 10 lb	A. Barclay

Won by 2 lengths, ¾ length.
4/9 Brigadier Gerard, 11/2 Hello, 8/1 Takasaki, 10/1 Comedy Star and Hill Command.

Time: 1 m 15.32 s

NEWMARKET, 1 October 1970

Middle Park Stakes, £10,515 18s., Bretby Stakes Course, 6 furlongs straight, two-year-old colts and fillies.

1	Brigadier Gerard, 9 st 0 lb	J. Mercer
2	Mummy's Pet, 9 st 0 lb	G. Lewis
3	Swing Easy (U.S.A.), 9 st 0 lb	L. Piggott
4	Fireside Chat (U.S.A.), 9 st 0 lb	A. Murray
5	Renoir Picture, 8 st 11 lb	B. Taylor

Won by 3 lengths, ½ length.
5/6 Mummy's Pet, 9/4 Swing Easy, 9/2 Brigadier Gerard, 100/8 Fireside Chat, 33/1 Renoir Picture.

Time: 1 m 15.11 s

NEWMARKET, 1 May 1971

The Two Thousand Guineas Stakes, £27,283.40, Rowley Mile, three-year-old colts and fillies.

1	Brigadier Gerard, 9 st o lb	J. Mercer
2	Mill Reef (U.S.A.), 9 st o lb	G. Lewis
3	My Swallow, 9 st o lb	F. Durr
4	Minsky (CAN), 9 st o lb	L. Piggott
5	Indian Ruler (U.S.A.), 9 st o lb	B. Taylor
6	Good Bond, 9 st o lb	J. Lindley

Won by 3 lengths, ¾ length.
6/4 Mill Reef, 2/1 My Swallow, 11/2 Brigadier Gerard, 15/2 Minsky, 16/1 Good Bond, 100/1 Indian Ruler.

Time: 1 m 39.20 s

ROYAL ASCOT, 15 June 1971

St James's Palace Stakes, £4,857.80, Old Mile, three-year-old colts and fillies.

1	Brigadier Gerard, 9 st o lb	J. Mercer
2	Sparkler, 9 st o lb	L. Piggott
3	Good Bond, 9 st o lb	A. Murray
4	Ballyhot, 9 st o lb	B. Taylor

Won by head, 6 lengths.
4/11 Brigadier Gerard, 3/1 Sparkler, 18/1 Good Bond, 33/1 Ballyhot.

Time: 1 m 46.94 s

GOODWOOD, 28 July 1971

Sussex Stakes, £12,134, Old Mile, three- and four-year-old colts and fillies.

1	Brigadier Gerard, 3, 8 st 7 lb	J. Mercer
2	Faraway Son (U.S.A.), 4, 9 st 4 lb	Y. Saint-Martin
3	Joshua, 4, 9 st 4 lb	G. Lewis
4	Ashleigh, 3, 8 st 7 lb	L. Piggott
5	King's Company, 3, 8 st 7 lb	F. Head

Won by 5 lengths, 2½ lengths.
4/6 Brigadier Gerard, 5/1 Faraway Son, 11/2 Ashleigh, 8/1 King's Company, 12/1 Joshua.

Time: 1 m 41.11 s

GOODWOOD, *28 August 1971*

Goodwood Mile, £3,926, Old Mile, three-year-olds and upwards.

1 Brigadier Gerard, 3, 8 st 6 lb	J. Mercer
2 Gold Rod, 4, 9 st 0 lb	L. Piggott
3 Ashleigh, 3, 8 st 1 lb	C. Roche

Won by 10 lengths, 4 lengths.
1/6 Brigadier Gerard, 6/1 Gold Rod, 14/1 Ashleigh.

Time: 1 m 42.07 s

ASCOT, *25 September 1971*

Queen Elizabeth II Stakes, £5,761, Old Mile, three-year-olds and upwards, entire colts and fillies.

1 Brigadier Gerard, 3, 8 st 8 lb	J. Mercer
2 Dictus (FR), 4, 9 st 1 lb	J. Taillard
3 Ashleigh, 3, 8 st 7 lb	L. Piggott

Won by 8 lengths, 10 lengths.
2/11 Brigadier Gerard, 6/1 Dictus, 22/1 Ashleigh.

Time: 1 m 41.39 s

NEWMARKET, *16 October 1971*

Champion Stakes, £25,279.60, 1 mile and 2 furlongs straight, three-year-olds and upwards, entire colts and fillies.

| 1 Brigadier Gerard, 3, 8 st 7 lb | J. Mercer |
| 2 Rarity, 4, 9 st 0 lb | P. Eddery |

3 Welsh Pageant, 5, 9 st 0 lb	G. Lewis
4 Gold Rod, 4, 9 st 0 lb	L. Piggott
5 Tamil, 4, 9 st 0 lb	W. Carson
6 Roi Soleil, 4, 9 st 0 lb	J. Lindley
7 Tratteggio, 3, 8 st 7 lb	F. Head
8 Amadou (FR), 4, 9 st 0 lb	H. Samani
9 Leander, 4, 9 st 0 lb	E. Eldin
10 Great Wall, 4, 9 st 0 lb	F. Durr

Won by a short head, 2½ lengths.
1/2 Brigadier Gerard, 17/2 Tratteggio, 9/1 Welsh Pageant, 13/1 Gold Rod, 16/1 Roi Soleil, 20/1 Rarity, 25/1 Amadou, 50/1 Great Wall, Tamil, 100/1 Leander.

Time: 2 m 17.09 s

NEWBURY, 20 May 1972

Lockinge Stakes, £7,249.65, 1 mile straight, for three-year-olds and upwards.

1 Brigadier Gerard, 4, 9 st 5 lb	J. Mercer
2 Grey Mirage, 3, 7 st 11 lb	R. Marshall
3 Gold Rod, 5, 9 st 5 lb	L. Piggott
4 Leander, 5, 8 st 12 lb	J. Lindley
5 Crespinall, 3, 7 st 9 lb	W. Carson

Won by 2½ lengths, 8 lengths.
1/4 Brigadier Gerard, 7/1 Grey Mirage, 14/1 Gold Rod, 33/1 Crespinall, 50/1 Leander.

Time: 1 m 41.44 s

SANDOWN, 29 May 1972

Westbury Stakes, £2,253.60, 1 mile and 2 furlongs, four-year-olds and upwards.

1 Brigadier Gerard, 4, 9 st 10 lb	J. Mercer
2 Ballyhot, 4, 8 st 10 lb	B. Taylor
3 Pembroke Castle, 5, 9 st 0 lb	G. Lewis
4 Fair World, 4, 9 st 0 lb	W. Carson
5 Juggernaut, 4, 9 st 0 lb	L. Piggott

Won by ½ length, 2 lengths.
4/11 Brigadier Gerard, 5/1 Pembroke Castle, 10/1 Ballyhot, 20/1 Juggernaut, 33/1 Fair World.

Time: 2 m 8.60 s

ROYAL ASCOT, 20 June 1972

Prince of Wales Stakes, £8,221.40, 1 mile and 2 furlongs, three-year-olds and upwards.

1	Brigadier Gerard, 4, 9 st 8 lb	J. Mercer
2	Steel Pulse, 3, 8 st 3 lb	E. Eldin
3	Pembroke Castle, 5, 9 st 4 lb	G. Lewis
4	Prominent, 5, 9 st 4 lb	G. Baxter
5	Lord David, 4, 9 st 2 lb	L. Piggott
6	The Broker, 3, 7 st 10 lb	W. Carson
7	Pardner, 3, 8 st 0 lb	G. McGrath

Won by 5 lengths, 1½ lengths.
1/2 Brigadier Gerard, 11/2 Lord David, 10/1 Steel Pulse, 16/1 Pembroke Castle, Prominent, 25/1 Pardner, 33/1 The Broker.

Time: 2 m 6.32 s (New course record)

SANDOWN, 8 July 1972

Eclipse Stakes, £32,579.75, one mile and two furlongs, three-year-olds and upwards, entire colts and fillies.

1	Brigadier Gerard, 4, 9 st 5 lb	J. Mercer
2	Gold Rod, 5, 9 st 5 lb	W. Carson
3	Home Guard (U.S.A.), 3, 8 st 7 lb	L. Piggott
4	Charladouce (FR), 4, 9 st 5 lb	B. Taylor
5	Alonso, 3, 8 st 7 lb	G. Lewis
6	Lord David, 4, 9 st 5 lb	A. Murray

Won by 1 length, 2 lengths.
4/11 Brigadier Gerard, 8/1 Home Guard, Lord David, 12/1 Alonso, 40/1 Charladouce, 50/1 Gold Rod.

Time: 2 m 20.20 s

ASCOT, 21 July 1972

King George VI and the Queen Elizabeth Stakes, £60,202, three-year-olds and upwards, entire colts and fillies.

1	Brigadier Gerard, 4, 9 st 7 lb	J. Mercer
2	Parnell, 4, 9 st 7 lb	W. Carson
3	Riverman (U.S.A.), 3, 8 st 7 lb	F. Head
4	Steel Pulse, 3, 8 st 7 lb	W. Williamson
5	Gay Lussac (ITY), 3, 8 st 7 lb	L. Piggott
6	Bog Road, 3, 8 st 7 lb	J. Lindley
7	Sukawa (FR), 3, 8 st 7 lb	Y. Saint-Martin
8	Selhurst, 4, 9 st 7 lb	G. Lewis
9	Fair World, 4, 9 st 7 lb	F. Durr

Won by 1½ lengths, 5 lengths.
8/13 Brigadier Gerard, 5/1 Gay Lussac, 17/2 Riverman, 12/1 Selhurst, 14/1 Steel Pulse, 28/1 Parnell, Sukawa, 66/1 others.

Time: 2 m 32.91 s

YORK, 15 August 1972

Benson and Hedges Gold Cup, £30,955, 1 mile, 2 furlongs and 110 yards, three-year-olds and upwards, entire colts and fillies.

1	Roberto (U.S.A.), 3, 8 st 10 lb	B. Baeza
2	Brigadier Gerard, 4, 9 st 7 lb	J. Mercer
3	Gold Rod, 5, 9 st 7 lb	W. Carson
4	Rheingold, 3, 8 st 10 lb	L. Piggott
5	Bright Beam, 5, 9 st 7 lb	G. Lewis

Won by 3 lengths, 10 lengths.
1/3 Brigadier Gerard, 7/2 Rheingold, 12/1 Roberto, 33/1 Gold Rod, 300/1 Bright Beam.

Time: 2 m 7.10 s (New course record)

ASCOT, 23 September 1972

Queen Elizabeth II Stakes, £5,658.50, Old Mile, three-year-olds and upwards, entire colts and fillies.

1 Brigadier Gerard, 4, 9 st 7 lb   J. Mercer
2 Sparkler, 4, 9 st 0 lb   L. Piggott
3 Redundant, 3, 8 st 7 lb   G. Lewis
4 Almagest, 5, 9 st 0 lb   J. Lindley

Won by 6 lengths, 5 lengths.
4/11 Brigadier Gerard, 3/1 Sparkler, 16/1 Redundant, 150/1 Almagest.

Time: 1 m 39.96 s (New course record)

NEWMARKET, 14 October 1972

Champion Stakes, £35,048.20, 1 mile and 2 furlongs straight, three-year-olds and upwards, entire colts and fillies.

1 Brigadier Gerard, 4, 9 st 3 lb   J. Mercer
2 Riverman (U.S.A.), 3, 8 st 10 lb   F. Head
3 Lord David, 4, 9 st 3 lb   G. Lewis
4 Jimsun, 3, 8 st 10 lb   J. Lindley
5 L'Apache, 4, 9 st 3 lb   E. Eldin
6 Boreen (FR), 4, 9 st 3 lb   R. F. Parnell
7 Sol 'Argent, 5, 9 st 3 lb   F. Durr
8 Almagest, 5, 9 st 3 lb   A. Murray
9 Steel Pulse, 3, 8 st 10 lb   W. Williamson

Won by 1½ lengths, 4 lengths.
1/3 Brigadier Gerard, 6/1 Riverman, 12/1 Boreen, 20/1 Steel Pulse, 33/1 Jimsun, Sol 'Argent, Lord David, 100/1 L'Apache, 500/1 Almagest.

Time: 2 m 7.41 s

Notes on the performances of Brigadier Gerard

He is the only English classic winner of the present century to have lost only one race in 18 or more starts.

He is the only English classic winner of the present century to have been unbeaten in ten or more starts at two and three years.

He is the only English classic winner of the present century to have won seven or more races as a four-year-old.

Only one other English classic winner of the present century has won the Eclipse Stakes and the Champion Stakes (twice) – Fairway.

Only two other English classic winners of the present century have won more races than Brigadier Gerard – Pretty Polly (22 races from 24 starts) and Bayardo (22 races from 25 starts).

Only two other English classic winners of the present century have won the Champion Stakes twice – Lemberg and Fairway.

He is the highest English-bred stakes winner of England and of Europe.

He holds the record for the Old Mile and for one and a quarter miles at Ascot.

Extract from Dick Hern's work book: Last Main Work of the Brigadier before the Two Thousand Guineas

Was on Saturday, 24 April 1971. Duration, L. Davies (7.3) Blks. Magnate, R. P. Elliot. Brigadier Gerard, J.M. Came 5 furlongs on trial ground. Magnate soon dropped away and Duration who had jumped off in front just held on from Brigadier Gerard. A very wet morning with the rain in their faces and ground on soft side.
J. Mercer was wearing a suede jacket which he weighed when he got home and found I think that he had been carrying an 8 lb penalty.

KEY MEN AT WEST ILSLEY
DURING BRIGADIER GERARD'S TIME

Major W. R. Hern	Trainer
J. Mercer	Stable jockey
B. Harrap	Secretary
R. (Geordie) Campbell	Head Lad
D. Bee	Second Head Lad
R. (Buster) Haslam	Head Travelling Lad
J. McCormack	Second Travelling Lad
R. Turner	Brigadier Gerard's exercise rider
L. Williamson	Brigadier Gerard's lad
R. Asher	Almagest's exercise rider
R. Cartwright	Work rider
B. Procter	Work rider
Tom Barnes	Feeder
Terry Barnes	Gallop man
D. Blyth	Blacksmith
P. West	Horse-box driver
R. Baggs	Night watchman

Brigadier Gerard's Total Earnings

1970	First	Second
Berkshire Stakes, Newbury	£1,201.00	
Champagne Stakes, Salisbury	£598.10	
Washington Singer Stakes, Newbury	£1,154.80	
Middle Park Stakes, Newmarket	£10,515.90	
	£13,469.80	

1971		
The Two Thousand Guineas, Newmarket	£27,283.40	
St James's Palace Stakes, Ascot	£4,857.80	
Sussex Stakes, Goodwood	£12,134.00	
Goodwood Mile, Goodwood	£3,926.00	
Queen Elizabeth II Stakes, Ascot	£5,761.00	
Champion Stakes, Newmarket	£25,279.60	
	£79,241.80	

1972		
Lockinge Stakes, Newbury	£7,249.65	
Westbury Stakes, Sandown	£2,253.60	
Prince of Wales Stakes, Ascot	£8,221.40	
Eclipse Stakes, Sandown	£32,579.75	
King George VI and the Queen Elizabeth Stakes, Ascot	£60,202.00	
Benson and Hedges Gold Cup, York		£9,100.00
Queen Elizabeth II Stakes, Ascot	£5,658.50	
Champion Stakes, Newmarket	£35,048.20	
	£151,213.10	Grand
Win Total:	£243,924.70	Total: £253,024.70

PRETTY POLLY ch. m. 1901	GALLINULE ch. 1884	ISONOMY b. 1875	STERLING	OXFORD	**BIRDCATCHER**	SIR HERCULES / GUICCOLI
					HONEY DEAR	PLENIPOTENTIARY / MY DEAR
				WHISPER	**FLATCATCHER**	TOUCHSTONE / DECOY
					SILENCE	MELBOURNE / SECRET
			ISOLA BELLA	**STOCKWELL**	**THE BARON**	**BIRDCATCHER** / ECHIDNA
					POCAHONTAS	GLENCOE / MARPESSA
				ISOLINE	ETHELBERT	FAUGH-A-BALLAGH / ESPOIR
					BASSISHAW	THE PRIME WARDEN / MISS WHINNEY
		MOORHEN br. 1873	HERMIT	NEWMINSTER	**TOUCHSTONE**	CAMEL / BANTER
					BEESWING	DR SYNTAX / Daughter of ARDROSSAN
				SECLUSION	TADMOR	ION / PALMYRA
					MISS SELLON	COWL / BELLE DAME
			Daughter of	SKIRMISHER	VOLTIGEUR	VOLTAIRE / MARTHA LYNN
					Daughter of	GARDHAM / Mare by LANGAR
				VERTUMNA	**STOCKWELL**	**THE BARON** / **POCAHONTAS**
					GARLAND	LANGAR / CAST STEEL
	ADMIRATION ch. 1892	SARABAND ch. 1883	MUNCASTER	DONCASTER	**STOCKWELL**	**THE BARON** / **POCAHONTAS**
					MARIGOLD	TEDDINGTON / Sister to SINGAPORE
				WINDERMERE	MACARONI	SWEETMEAT / JOCOSE
					MISS AGNES	**BIRDCATCHER** / AGNES
			HIGHLAND FLING	SCOTTISH CHIEF	LORD OF THE ISLES	**TOUCHSTONE** / FAIR HELEN
					MISS ANN	LITTLE KNOWN / BAY MISSY
				MASQUERADE	LAMBOURNE	LOUP GAROU / Sister to SATIRIST
					BURLESQUE	**TOUCHSTONE** / MAID OF HONOUR
		GAZE b. 1886	THURINGIAN PRINCE	THORMANBY	WINDHOUND	PANTALOON / PHRYNE
					ALICE HAWTHORN	MULEY MOLOCH / REBECCA
				EASTERN PRINCESS	SURPLICE	**TOUCHSTONE** / CRUCIFIX
					TOMYRIS	SESOSTRIS / SANBOY'S Dam
			EYE PLEASER	BROWN BREAD	WEATHERBIT	SHEET ANCHOR / MISS LETTY
					BROWN AGNES	WEST AUSTRALIAN / MISS AGNES
				WALLFLOWER	RATAPLAN	**THE BARON** / **POCAHONTAS**
					CHAPERON	**FLATCATCHER** / Mare by PANTALOON

BRIGADIER GERARD b.c. 1968						
	QUEEN'S HUSSAR b. 1960	MARCH PAST br. 1950	PETITION	**FAIR TRIAL**	**FAIRWAY**	**PHALARIS** / SCAPA FLOW
					LADY JUROR	SON-IN-LAW / LADY JOSEPHINE
				ART PAPER	ARTIST'S PROOF	GAINSBOROUGH / CLEAR EVIDENCE
					QUIRE	FAIRY KING / QUEEN CARBINE
			MARCELETTE	WILLIAM OF VALENCE	VATOUT	PRINCE CHIMAY / VASTHI
					QUEEN ISEULT	TEDDY / SWEET AGNES
				PERMAVON	STRATFORD	SWYNFORD / LESBIA
					CURL PAPER	**PAPYRUS** / COILA
		JOJO gr. 1950	VILMORIN	GOLD BRIDGE	SWYNFORD of GOLDEN BOSS	THE BOSS / GOLDEN HEN
					FLYING DIADEM	DIADUMENOS / FLYING BRIDGE
				QUEEN OF THE MEADOWS	**FAIRWAY**	**PHALARIS** / SCAPA FLOW
					QUEEN OF THE BLUES	BACHELOR'S DOUBLE / BLUE FAIRY
			FAIRY JANE	**FAIR TRIAL**	**FAIRWAY**	**PHALARIS** / SCAPA FLOW
					LADY JUROR	SON-IN-LAW / LADY JOSEPHINE
				LIGHT TACKLE	SALMON TROUT	THE TETRARCH / SALAMANDRA
					TRUE JOY	STEDFAST / JOYZELLE
	LA PAIVA ch. 1956	PRINCE CHEVALIER b. 1943	PRINCE ROSE	ROSE PRINCE	PRINCE PALATINE	**PERSIMMON** / LADY LIGHTFOOT
					EGLANTINE	PERTH / ROSE DE MAI
				INDOLENCE	GAY CRUSADER	BAYARDO / GAY LAURA
					BARRIER	GREY LEG / BAR THE WAY
			CHEVALERIE	ABBOT'S SPEED	ABBOT'S TRACE	**TRACERY** / ABBOTT'S ANNE
					MARY GAUNT	JOHN O' GAUNT / QUICK
				KASSALA	CYLGAD	**CYLLENE** / GADFLY
					FARIZADE	SARDANAPALE / DIAVOLEZZA
		BRAZEN MOLLY b. 1940	HORUS	**PAPYRUS**	**TRACERY**	ROCK SAND / TOPIARY
					MISS MATTY	MARCOVIL / SIMONATH
				LADY PEREGRINE	WHITE EAGLE	GALLINULE / MERRY GAL
					LISMA	**PERSIMMON** / LUSCIOUS
			MOLLY ADARE	**PHALARIS**	POLYMELUS	**CYLLENE** / MAID MARIAN
					BROMUS	SAINFOIN / CHEERY
				MOLLY DESMOND	DESMOND	ST SIMON / L'ABBESSE DE JOUARRE
					PRETTY POLLY	GALLINULE / ADMIRATION

Index

[*Names of horses are in italic*]